THE SWORDS OF WORDS

A Mother and Daughter's Battle
to a Miraculous Restoration

KRISTY ORISON

ISBN:
Paperback: 978-164746-971-9
Hardback: 978-1-64746-972-6
EBook: 978-1-64746-973-3

Library of Congress Control Number: 2021924051

A TRIBUTE TO MY MOTHER

Thank you for all that your life and death have taught me.

Every year, on March 8th, I celebrate your birth along with International Women's Day. It is no coincidence that you shared your birthday with that national holiday. You were a strong woman, in many ways that I failed to recognize…until the end.

Barbara Pitts

March 8, 1939 – August 19, 2015
Life is brief. The end marked by a little dash…
a horizontal line that marks time.
If only that dash could speak!

Table of Contents

PART 1: THE PIT

1. Missing You 1
2. Christmas Memories 8
3. A Memorial 17

PART 2: THE PRISON

4. Can't We All Get Along? 27
5. Her Softer Side. 37
6. Her Illness 47

PART 3: THE PROMISE

7. Her Final Days. 60
8. The Hole In My Heart. 67
9. He Restores 78
10. Reprise 82
11. Thoughts, Scripture Meditations, and a Prayer 95

Acknowledgements 109
End Notes 113
Endorsements. 117

• • • | • • •

Missing You

YESTERDAY'S A CLOSING door…. I don't live there any-more. I am trying to say goodbye to where I have been…. I am trying to get my heart to beat again!![1]

Dear Mom, 9-30-17

I am sitting on a fall day in a park…I wish you were sitting here with me, as I know you would love it here. The leaves are starting to turn and there is nothing but incredible nature all around me. That's something I so learned from you… to enjoy the peace and solitude of the great outdoors. I miss you! I thought I would never hear myself say that. For years, I longed for you to go away. The shame and heartache of having a mother that was so hard to get close to and feel connected to; made my heart ache. I felt that if you went away, my life would be easier, and I would not be reminded of the hard childhood and home life that I had for so many years. The reason it has gotten so much easier is not because you are gone...but because I have found incredible peace in being alone and living alone.

I used to think that I did not want to spend the rest of my life alone, like you did. I did not want to be at the end of my life and not have a significant other to be there for me. In my quest for this, I completely lost myself in a few relationships these last 6 years, especially in the last couple of years after losing you. If you were here and we were having this conversation... you would tell me, I am sure, how much you loved being alone. Yes, you got lonely, but your solitude was a very peaceful existence for you, as it is for me now. So, thank you for that lesson! I see how much of that I have probably inherited from you. And that is not a bad thing. I am sorry for thinking that it was not good for you. I guess, I just wish that you would not have had to be so fearful at times when you were alone and doing everything on your own...especially as your mind and body started to deteriorate. How frightening that must have been for you, to wonder if you would be able to live on your own and take care of yourself. You were such an incredibly strong woman, but even in the midst of your fragile state toward the end, you were going to fight to be on your own and not depend on anyone. I get that now. I really, really get that!

I am in Nashville, TN this weekend and heading to the Grand Old Opry tonight. I know you would have loved to come here and go to the Opry. You so loved country music. I wish you could have done all the things you always wanted to do. Maybe that is why my bucket list is so much of a priority for me. I now realize that unless you intentionally get up and go do these things...your 'someday' may never come.

I wish I would have taken more time to go do the things you loved with you. Or even taken the time to call or better yet... should have written to you. You were fabulous at letter writing and I so cherish those letters. Even if some of them were not so kind! You had something to say. You needed to express

2

yourself and the pen and paper were your outlet. I understand that now. Oh, the lessons that come with loss and time.

I miss you! Will write more later.

Love,
Kristy

Returning to places I have been before always brings reflective moments for me. So it was as I returned to Nashville, as I had been there a few times before. Eight years earlier, my husband at the time and I came to a place called ONSITE. It is a sacred place of healing, about an hour north of Nashville, with several different clinic-based therapeutic workshops. We had been in counseling for several years and we were really struggling with some issues in our marriage, and Onsite was recommended to us by our therapist. I was kicking and screaming the whole way there. I had spent so much time in recovery and therapy, digging up my issues, that I did not want to go start all over again with another therapist or workshop! But once I got there, I fell in love with the whole experiential process. And fell in love with the beautiful countryside, as well.

The couple's workshop we did at Onsite did help with some of the communication issues in our marriage. Unfortunately, about a year and a half later, there was still so much damage that we had both done to the relationship that we separated. I then found myself back at Onsite doing their "Healing the Trauma Within' program. My therapist had recommended that I attend this workshop for the deep trauma I had experienced in my childhood. The trauma of the divorce of my parents shortly after I was born. The trauma of growing up without knowing my father, as we moved away from him and his family and I didn't see them again for many years. The trauma of being raised by my stepfather, who I really, really disliked, and a mother who had alcoholic issues and some mental issues from her own childhood abuse!

3

So, I came to Onsite again. I did not come kicking and screaming this time. I came with hope and love in my heart for what healing and insight was in store for me. When they detoxed us from the world for the first couple of days, I was all in for handing in my cell phone and abstaining from social media. I welcomed that and looked forward to the challenge of diving into whatever God was going to have come my way once the distractions were eliminated. I loved the country there of acres and acres of trees, winding roads, sprawling ranches, and grazing horses.

The first couple of days were really opportunities for the group leader to help each of us build trust with the other members in our group. One of the first exercises was to draw your trauma experience. We were given a few minutes to think and reflect on this. As the counselor was speaking, my vision came.

I was about to celebrate my seventh birthday! My birthday happens to land on Christmas Day. I always hated this! My mother tried to make it special for me, as she would separate my presents by wrapping them in 'birthday' paper and letting me open my birthday presents first, before anyone else opened their Christmas presents. She also made sure I always had a special cake for my birthday. We were quite poor, growing up in a small Nebraska town, so these gestures were as special as she could do.

It was Christmas Eve, 1968, and my stepfather had stopped at the corner bar on his way home from work as he often did. He announced in a very drunken, loud voice that we were opening presents that night, rather than waiting until Christmas Day as we had always done. This threw my mother into a bit of a rage. She blew back at him that none of the presents were wrapped and that we are not changing this. A tug of war between them began as it often did when one or both were drinking. My stepfather won!

The presents were all hidden in a closet right off the living room where we all sat that Christmas Eve. I was anxious, as I never liked when either of them had been drinking and did

4

not like the uncertainty of things as they escalated. I was also excited to get to open presents early. But if the presents were not wrapped, how would I know which presents were for my birthday or for Christmas?

It turned out to be ugly…truly, truly ugly! My mother went to the closet and started throwing the unwrapped presents at all of us. There was no surprise or anticipation in what the presents were. There was just anger and drunkenness and disappointment for everyone. At the end of her angry rage of throwing presents, I sat there wearing my new big furry hat that dangled with furry tassels and cried uncontrollably. I was screaming, "I hate my birthday being on Christmas, I hate my birthday being on Christmas! It's not fair!"

"It is not my fault! You were not supposed to be born until the end of February. Your father came home Christmas Eve drunk with his new girlfriend, a fight began, and he threw me down a flight of stairs and you were born. You should have died…you should have died….and you are damn lucky to be alive!"

"Death and Life are in the power of the tongue".[2]

Those words felt like a sword piercing my heart. Something happened to me after that. The happy, hopeful little girl in me died. My heart and mind decided right then and there that I would never ask for anything or depend on anyone again. I realized what a burden I was to my mother and the pain that my birth had caused her. And possibly in her rage, did she wish that I had died?

> "Death and life are in the power of the tongue."

My stepfather coming home drunk on Christmas Eve 1968 had caused a Post-Traumatic Stress moment in my mother, and the whole scene now gave her an opportunity to dump her pain on me. As a needy little girl, I took it on, and on, and on, and on.

I then wrote my own lyrics to the song, "Please Daddy Don't Get Drunk This Christmas" I don't want to see my momma cry...that year when I was only seven, you did, and it made this little girl want to die.

Now here I was, 40 years later, in a room at Onsite with four other women and a counselor, seeing this whole scene in my mind and being challenged to draw my trauma with crayons. It was a simple drawing...a Christmas tree, me with my big furry hat on, and my mother throwing presents.

Music began to play. The tenderness and words of the song tore 40 years of my heart wide open, and I could do nothing but once again sob uncontrollably! I was back in that moment. Feeling seven again...along with every horrifying feeling my heart had held on to for all those years. The deep infection of fear, rejection, and abandonment started to ooze out of me as the song, "How could anyone ever tell you...you were anything less than beautiful...How could anyone ever tell you...you were less than whole" by Shaina Noll[3] continued to play.

No, no one has ever told me I was beautiful, no one has ever told me I was whole. No one has ever told me I am a miracle. If they have, I could not hear it! My ears were only in tune to the words...you are damn lucky to be alive...you should have died.

For last year's words belong to last year's language and this year's words await another voice. To make an end is to make a beginning...[4]

This was my new beginning! A safe place with four other women who each had similar trauma experiences. All of us coming together to unveil the wound, to try and trust again, and, more than anything, to allow our hearts to heal and beat again. The process was painful but nothing less than miraculous how God showed up. As I was explaining my drawing of my trauma, the eyes of the woman across from me grew very large and deeply connected to mine. As each of our stories unfolded, we bonded over our many common connections. We were both born on Christmas Day, and our mothers had traumatic experiences at our births. Her name was Mary, which really blew me away, as my name was going to be Mary Noel--- a festive name for a

Christmas baby. I am grateful my mother changed her mind and named me Kristy!

I am so deeply moved by how the good Lord could bring two women, similar in age, with similar spirits and hearts. One traveling to Nashville from the Midwest and the other coming all the way from the UK to come together for such a time of healing as this!

...2...

Christmas Memories

Even if my Father and Mother abandon me, the Lord will hold me close. (PS 27:10, NKJ)

Dear Mom,   **12-25-17**

Merry Christmas!! It has been two and a half years since you passed away, and I am still missing you. Going to try and write to you even though the tears are so strong, and my heart still aches. Christmas and my birthday have always been hard since the year I learned of your pain in bringing me into the world. My heart hurts for how traumatic that must have been for you that Christmas. To be alone, as my father was with another woman. You were now going be a single mom, raising three children on your own. The day should have been a joyful time for you, not just because it was Christmas, but because you were about to give life again. The very thing that God made a woman for, to be the giver of life! But another life for you meant a bigger burden to care for. I am sorry you had to bear that alone.

As you know, I use to feel so sorry for myself for being born on Christmas because I hated having everyone else get gifts the same day I did. I wanted it to be special for me…just for me! It has taken me years to realize that my selfishness in this was okay. We are all born with some form of self-centeredness. That is why we need a Savior, why we need Christmas, why we need the reminder that it is about giving. The perfect gift was given to us that first Christmas morn. I no longer hate that I was born on Christmas, but I hate that it brought you great pain, and I hate the mess I was born in.

That mess has been such a stronghold in my life since my first breath! The sins of our fathers will be passed on to the third and fourth generations. Adultery, divorce, abandonment, alcoholism, and abuse are all threads in the tapestry of my life that I no longer want to weave with. I have just gone through yet another male relationship that, for the umpteenth time, took me around that painful mountain. I pray… Please, Lord…help me to learn my lesson well this time, as I don't want to take this test again. I am so tired and weary and beyond sick and tired of being sick and tired from this pain. This is a giant in my life, a giant that is no match for God… but why, oh why, do I have to keep experiencing this? Why do I keep compromising and losing myself in some man?

I witnessed this same pattern in you, and I understand why you did it. It was a different era for you, trying to survive as a single mom with limited resources. I, however, do not need to do that anymore. I do not need someone to take care of me or support me. I do not need to be on someone's arm or have their approval or belong to someone's family to know that I am loved and have worth as a single person. I embrace my singleness as a gift from God.

My life verse for these relationships has been Proverbs 10:10. "He who winks with an eye causes trouble." I watched you wink with that eye many times in your relationships with the men in your life. I am not blaming you for passing that on to me. You did not know any different. I wish I knew what had happened to you that you so compromised yourself in these relationships and did not walk away and know your worth. I have spent years trying to understand my own insanity in this. My guess is that you experienced some of the same things that I have experienced. My hope and prayer is for the generations to follow me—my son, my grandchildren, and all who follow them—will not have to go through a lot of the same pain. That is my driving force for writing to you, writing this, and digging into this mess. They say that your mess can become your message!

I know if you were here today and could unveil the joy, peace, and forgiveness you have found in heaven, you would be giving me wisdom. I am saddened that you did not find more of that here on earth. My quest is to not learn this too late! To starve these distractions in my life and feed my focus. Your exit from this world has taught me so much. I am alone this Christmas and am more at peace than I ever have been. It is a painful peace sometimes, as it takes me to a deeper place—a place where being alone with the Lord allows me to reflect on what this life is really all about and what my purpose is. I believe it is to be an instrument of peace, to love more than I am loved, and to forgive. To really forgive and to give God the glory for all He has brought me through. I may not do this perfectly, but it is my prayer.

> To starve these distractions in my life and feed my focus.

Last night, I had such a fabulous memory of you from when I was a little girl. We were traveling to friends on Christmas Eve. I was lying on your lap, looking up at the stars, and you were singing "Silent Night." It was such a soft, tender sweet voice. I loved that voice…and needed to hear that voice again.

That needs to be the voice I remember, not the loud, angry voice that shouted, "You're damn lucky to be alive!"

It is turning out to be a lovely Christmas and birthday! Amazing how things come full circle and God will restore the years that the locust has eaten. The last six months have been painful from a deceiving relationship. But it was good that I was afflicted, as I now feel that this will push me closer to my destiny. For it was Judas Iscariot's betrayal, rather than Peter's faithful love, that got Jesus closer to His destiny on the cross. I pray it for me, as well.

I am checking things off my bucket list. Taking trips alone, working on my book. The greatest joy this year was that finally, after 50 years of so wanting a pony, I got one! It is just like the one I have always dreamed of since I was a little girl. I remember going back to Idaho to visit Grandma and Grandpa a few years after we left. I was about five years old. Uncle Craig took us to the Pocatello Rodeo and introduced me to his love for horses. It is the only memory I have of Idaho and my father's family as a child. I have dreamed of having a horse ever since. But not just any horse. The horse had to have the Orison blonde mane. I have saved pictures of what he would look like for years and had an artist several years ago do a life-size portrait of this dream horse. After leaving Onsite seven years ago, I even went and bought a little stuffed chestnut pony with a blonde mane. I have held and cried and cried with that little guy many a night. That is what they taught me in the workshop I did on healing my trauma within. That horse represented so much of that Christmas Day I was born in Idaho! So, it is only fitting that my new little pony should be named Idaho.

He is a rescue pony who was abandoned and abused and now suffers from a lot of fear and is very timid. He is not very tall, so he will have to overcome that along with his fear issues. He is a haflinger with a little Arab in him, so he's a very strong mountain pack horse, much like the Orison family men I knew. The beautiful flaxen color of his mane and tail is a true Orison trait.

I really wanted a rescue horse, as it represents my own rescue in this life. The abandonment by my father, which is my deepest wound, put me in a search for a father figure and the love and acceptance I so desperately needed from him. Unfortunately, it has taken me too many times to try and find this in all the wrong places. In a church service I attended as a child, I heard the pastor speak about God being the "father to the fatherless". I think this was the first seed that was planted in me to yearn and search for Him, and it eventually led me, one day, to bow my head and claim Jesus as the Lord and Savior of my life.

My old nature still rears its ugly head occasionally. I may, at times, go back and slightly dip my toe into the pig pen and roll in the mud once in a while, but it is not my default anymore, and I do not stay there! My heart now yearns to be different. The Good Shephard now reminds me who I am in Him…I hear His voice and love how He leads and restores me to Him when I have strayed. I want to be that same kind of leader to my horse now. He belongs to me. There is no need for him to live in the fear and state of abandonment, not knowing who he can trust or who he belongs to. He has high standards for anyone who comes near him, as he should! He has been roughed up and abused, and he is not going to let anyone come close to him unless he has complete trust that they are not going to hurt him! I love what he is teaching me. Horses bond with the hand that leads them, so I am going to put my heart and soul into this horse. I have tried to rescue and clean up so many men and failed miserably! I'm hoping horses will be far more rewarding.

I wish you were here to meet him. You would love him. I miss you, Mom. Thank you for bringing me into this world, as painful as it was for you. I should have said this many years ago.

I am overjoyed to be alive. Overjoyed to have had the mess. For without the mess, I would have never met the messenger!

My Grown-up Christmas List: No more lives torn apart. Time would heal the heart. Everyone would have a friend and love would never end![5]

Merry Christmas!

Love you,
Kristy

CHRISTMAS ONCE AGAIN brings reflection back to that painful Christmas Eve of 1968 when I was seven, but the memory is different now, after the work I did at Onsite. As Mary and I sat on the floor in a bit of awe over our similar stories and traumas at birth, I felt a tenderness towards her and what she had gone through. It got me out of myself and my pity party about my own trauma, and a sweet sense of healing began. I felt that her experience was far more traumatic than mine, and my heart really ached for her. She had suffered a physical disability in her hands from her birth, and her mother neglected her throughout her life because of it.

We bonded and continued throughout the week to find more and more similarities in our personalities. Our starvation for attention and acceptance was a result of the lack of bonding our parents were able to give us at birth and as children. We both had turned, of course, to male relationships to try and fill this void. We both had married men much older than we were, seeking that lost love from a father figure. We both had incidents in our teens where we were sexually abused by our brother's friends… and those incidents both happened one day in the woods.

These were the moments at Onsite that took my breath away. How do you explain moments like this? I felt that I had met what feels like my twin sister. The paths that she and I had walked were eerily close. Meeting her like this, and listening to her story unfold alongside mine, made my heart leap. I knew now that I was not alone. There was someone else out there who gets me. Someone else out there who has embraced a painful rejection at birth and made unhealthy decisions because of it, and who now has a heart that wants to heal. The sweetest moment I remember of my connection with Mary was that, in spite of her disability in her hands, she was a writer. And I, for many years, had wanted to be a writer. Mary became my hero!

So, our therapist at Onsite took us both back "into the woods." Individually, we set the stage for each of our stories and re-played the scenes. A heaviness comes over my chest just thinking about this. I have undergone hypnosis and endured countless moments of a therapist trying to bring me back to this moment to unlock what happened that day, but I had never had any breakthroughs. I only remember a few details of it. I truly believe that is a God thing! He puts a protection around our brains to not allow us to go back and remember something that is too painful for us to bear. It is like spiritual amnesia.

The blessing that day at Onsite was that the therapist was not trying to take me back to relive it. We were just setting the scene with experiential therapy. It began with all the characters standing in the woods together. Myself, my brother, and my brother's friend, Wally. (Wally actually wasn't my brother's friend...he was the neighbor's grandson, who came to town every few months and would come over and play catch on occasion with my brother). I am not sure how we ended up in the woods behind our house...but we did! I really do not remember the details of what happened there, but I do remember the smells of the incident. The smell of an obnoxious weed on the ground... to this day, when I smell it, I call it the Wally Weed. And then I remember smelling semen, or as I called it for many years after that, the smell of sex. (As I was only 11 years old at the time, I really did not know what semen was.)

Our safe group members at Onsite became the characters who were present that day. I was myself, and two of the other girls acted out the parts of my brother and Wally. Once I told the story as far as I could tell it, it was time for me to choose a different ending. How should this have ended? Ideally, I would have loved my brother to have protected me from Wally. I do not remember what happened that he did not…I think he may have left us. So, who should have protected me? And if my brother was still there, who should have protected both of us from this bully? My mother? My father? My grandfather?

My mother and stepfather were in their own mess of pain and numbness, with a bitter marriage and lots of alcohol. I believe my mother had experiences like my day in the woods with her own brothers. There was no way she was emotionally able to be there to protect me, as she was still living in her own shame and lack of ability to protect herself, let alone her daughter.

I stood in deep thought about all of this and suddenly wanted no one other than my grandfather! He should have been there for me…he should have protected me and my brother. The scene was set, and all of us were playing our parts. Wally was bullying me sexually. I do not remember where my brother was, so he was now just a passive figure in the scene. I was afraid and frozen in my fear! And in the midst of our little one act play, along came my big teddy bear grandfather. My papa bear, who stood up to Wally. He gave him a threat or two about coming near his grandchildren and what he was going to do to him if he even so much as laid a hand on either of us.

It was so powerful! The woman who played my grandfather was miraculous in her delivery and her healing words, hugs, and love towards me. That is how the story should have ended. And with that, my mind and my heart saw this whole horrible ordeal in a totally different light. It was all going to be okay. It was not anybody's fault that they were not there for me. Nor was it my fault that this happened to me. There had been generations of "winking with an eye" and allowing trouble and evil to come into our families, creating generational curses with these strongholds in our lives. When I felt the love and protection from my grandfather, who I wished would have been there for me that day, the awful memory of the scene in the woods disappeared behind all the big, beautiful trees. It left behind a memory of the smell of lush green grass, a fresh breeze, and a ray of sunshine!

For how does one explain the love of God? To block my memory for so many years and then to replace it with an enduring thought of a grandfather's love and protection. "The Lord's mercies are new every morning, Great is your faithfulness!" (Lam: 3:22 NKJ)

Love you Grandpa.

...3...

A Memorial

"Do not fear, for you will not be ashamed; neither be disgraced, for you will not be put to shame; for you will forget the shame of your youth and will not remember the reproach of your widowhood anymore." (IS 54:4 NKJ)

IT IS MEMORIAL Day, and I am remembering my mom. The memories are very different now. I am grateful that I am reminded of the good she brought to the world, of her sacrifice as a young woman to our country when she served in the Armed Forces. I enjoyed listening to her stories regarding that period in her life. It was many, many years ago, long before there were very many women who served in the Military. I cannot remember what she did exactly, but I do know it had to do with her typing and writing skills. I always marveled at her penmanship and her letters. I have kept many of them.

I was always fearful when one of her letters came, as I did not know what to expect. She vented a lot in her letters, and they could be pretty harsh. Looking back, I love to have the memory of her handwriting and the memory of her thoughts in the form of these letters. They hurt and paralyzed me many times, as I so desperately wanted her approval and did not want to be attacked or blamed for something that I could not defend myself from. I often had no idea of what prompted her letters or the things she would accuse me of. They were often the basis for much drama and division in our family. That saddens me to this day. Nonetheless, it was her "safe" way to communicate. So, now I am writing her back.

Do I wish I had written back when she was alive? It is hard to say. On the one hand, her letters left me pretty speechless. On the other hand, she had often expressed to me how much writing and receiving letters meant to her. There were too many times that I could not give myself a voice. I would receive her letters and keep it all in. I would pray about whatever was said in the letter and process and feel the feelings it brought about, but I usually didn't want to respond. This was the passive little girl in me who felt a lot of hurt and shame and wished things could have been different for her, for me, for our family. Even if the letters were full of joy or good news or just talking about her day or the weather or her animals, I just took it all in and kept my distance. I found the up and down moods reflected in her letters very untrustworthy and hard to get close to. About the time I would let my heart soften and get connected to her and feel like she approved of me, a letter would come that would stab my heart and attack the core of my being, leaving me wounded, hurt, and wanting to retreat to my safe "alone" place. It's like the story my therapist told me years ago about the tortoise and the porcupine:

Once upon a time, there was a little porcupine. He was a very strange looking creature because although he had quite a small body, it was covered from head to foot with many long fierce-looking quills, and they stuck up all around his body, even when they were lying down, so the little porcupine looked three times his real size. And that was very useful to him because when he would go walking out of his burrow where he lived, he noticed that other animals and birds, much larger than he, would stop when they saw him and give him space as he passed. He thought that was very funny, but also, he felt a little sad because he felt quite lonely, and he didn't know any other porcupines. And so, he had to spend a lot of time alone.

When he walked, he saw that other creatures seemed to be afraid of him and that seemed very strange to him because HE was afraid of THEM! As a matter of fact, if there would be a sudden loud noise, or some creature would come up behind him suddenly, then without trying at all, every quill on his body would stand straight up, and he would look not just three times his size, but ten times his size, and other creatures would back off.

Sometimes, they would say to him, "My goodness, you're fierce. My goodness, you're an angry one. Why are you so angry?" And the little porcupine was puzzled because he didn't feel angry at all. He just felt scared. And he did notice that from time to time when some foolish creature would get too close, his quills would stick in them, and they would run off screeching and hollering and crying when he had done nothing but stand still. Other creatures accused him of shooting his quills at them. It wasn't true at all. This was puzzling and so his days passed, and he felt very confused and very lonely and quite bored being by himself.

One day, as he was walking in the forest, as usual going his own lonely way, he met a huge turtle. The turtle stopped and looked at him and said, "My goodness, you're a strange looking one." And Porky raised up all his quills at once because he felt very afraid. And the turtle said, "That is amazing! You can make yourself ten times your size whereas all I can do is pull my head and feet in and make myself smaller."

"Oh," said the porcupine, "let me see!" And so the turtle obligingly pulled his head in and pulled in his feet, and, in fact, he was much smaller. Not only that, he looked so much like the rocks and stones all about him that the porcupine had to look very closely to see which one was the turtle.

"My," said the porcupine, "I wish I could pull in my head and feet and make myself into a stone." And the turtle peeked out and said, "Oh, I wish I could make myself ten times as big and have those fierce looking spears all over me, instead of having to pull in and be like a stone. It's dark in there and very boring."

"Well," said the porcupine, "you know something? I am bored, too, because with my making myself ten times as big as I am and sticking out my fierce looking quills, all other creatures avoid me."

"Well," said the turtle, "that's very strange. I wouldn't want to avoid you. Why do they avoid you?"

"Well, "said the porcupine, "if they come near, they get hurt."

"Ha ha ha ha," said the turtle. "I can come near." And he did. And the little porcupine began to shake because no other creature had ever come so close. And the turtle said, "See, I can even touch you." And he did.

The porcupine backed off and said, "Ooh, don't touch me! Nobody has ever touched me!"

But the turtle said, "I can touch you."

And the porcupine said, "So you can. And my quills don't stick into you."

"Oh, no," said the turtle, "because I have this beautiful shell. See my beautiful shell? You have your quills and I have my shell, and those protect us because inside we're really soft and very scared." And the little porcupine began to laugh because he had found a friend who understood exactly how he felt and was not afraid of his quills, and he was not afraid of the turtle because the turtle was not afraid of him: and do you know, they became very good friends.

Then the little porcupine began to understand that everyone else was afraid like him, and so he learned to keep his quills sleek against his body even though his heart was beating very hard. And every time after, when he would meet a new creature, he kept his fierce-looking quills sleek against his body, so he looked only three times his real size instead of ten times. And he learned to say, "Are you afraid? Because I'm afraid too, but all I want to do is play. Is that what you want?"

And do you know, the next time he met a little chipmunk, the chipmunk said, "Yes, that's how I feel, too. Do you mean that you won't shoot your spears at me if I come close?"

"Of course not," said the porcupine, "and anyway, I can't shoot any spears. I can only make them stand up, and you get stuck if you come too close when I am afraid."

"Oh," said the chipmunk, "you don't have to be afraid of me. All I can do is scratch and bite and there is no place on you at all where I could bite or scratch. You don't have to be afraid of me, and if you won't stick me with your quills, I don't have to be afraid of you."

"That's right," said the porcupine, and he laughed out loud with pleasure, and do you know, soon the little porcupine was friends with everyone in the forest.

One day, a surly big creature came into the forest. No one had ever seen anyone like him before. When he laughed it sounded like a snarl, and when he snarled, he sounded even worse, and he was very ugly, although no one wanted him to know that they thought so. He had long front legs and sort of crouching, cringing back legs, and he had ugly rough fur in patches, and a long mean snout and long snaggly teeth. This creature came swaggering up to where the little porcupine was standing with all his quills sleek against his body. The little porcupine said, "Hello," in a quavering voice. The creature laughed his laugh which sounded like a snarl, and the little porcupine asked, "What is your name?"

The creature said, "What's it to ya?"

"Oh," said the little porcupine, "my name is Porky." And the creature laughed like a snarl again. "And I would like to know your name," said Porky.

"Oh, well, all right, nosey," he said. "My name is Laughing Hyena."

"Oh," said Porky, "that's an interesting name."

"You making fun of me?" snarled the hyena, and Porky cried, "Oh, no sir, no sir. Not at all, sir."

"Well," said the laughing hyena, "you'd better not because I could just make mincemeat outta you in one bite." Little Porky's quills stood straight up, and the laughing hyena said, "Oh, you wanna fight, do ya? Well, I'll show you." And so he jumped at little Porky, and little Porky stood there shaking all over like a thistle in the wind. And do you know what happened? That mean laughing hyena got his long mean snout stuck full of quills and there were quills sticking in his ears and all over his ugly body. He put his tail between his legs and ran off howling hideously, straight out of the forest.

Then all the creatures applauded and said, "Oh, Porky, you were wonderful." And Porky said, "Well, I really didn't do anything. And I feel bad now because I did what I have just learned not to do. I have *learned not to scare off everyone, and to realize that everyone is scared of me."*

"That's all right, Porky," they said. "There are times when you have to use what you have to protect yourself, but most of the time you just have to be friends." And little Porky felt glad in his heart because from then on, he knew the difference between making friends and protecting himself.[6]

● ● ●

It has taken me years to learn to NOT retreat into my turtle shell. The quills that came in the form of her letters stuck in me and the verbal attacks over the years left me pierced and wounded. The piercing words echoed so much that I could not hear or let the positive words and affirmations in.

"You will speak profoundly someday"
> "You are damn lucky to be alive…you should
> have died"

"You are a beautiful woman"
> "You are damn lucky to be alive…you should
> have died"

"You are so talented"
> "You are damn lucky to be alive…you should
> have died"

"You are a child of God"
> "You are damn lucky to be alive…you should
> have died"

"You will do great things"
> "You are damn lucky to be alive…you should
> have died"

"God has a purpose and plan for your life"
> "You are damn lucky to be alive…you should
> have died"

"You will find someone who will love and accept you for who you are"

>"You are damn lucky to be alive…you should have died"

"The Lord will never leave you, nor forsake you"

>"You are damn lucky to be alive…you should have died"

"You have the most beautiful hair"

>"You are damn lucky to be alive…you should have died"

"You have such a beautiful heart and spirit"

>"You are damn lucky to be alive….you should have died"

No, I am not damn lucky to be alive! No, I should not have died!

Those are the words of the enemy, the words of his sword that wants to kill, steal, and destroy. But God has got this. His hand has always been on my life. For by His grace, I have lived through the abandonment of my father, suicide attempts on my life, a pregnancy outside of marriage, being a single mom for several years, and a divorce.

My life was not at the mercy of my mother and father and the physical circumstances that brought me into this world. My days are numbered and in His hands. I am not damn lucky to be alive. I was predestined and He knew me before I was knitted in my mother's womb. "For who He foreknew He also predestined to be conformed to the likeness of His son that he might be the firstborn among many brethren." (Romans 8:29 NKJ) He knew the moment I would take my first breath and He knows the time of my final breath. He has a plan and a purpose for my life. Plans to prosper me and for harm not to come to me. Plans to give me a hope and a future…so that when I come to Him, He will answer! When I seek Him, I will find Him…when I seek Him with all my heart, I will be found by Him....! (Jer 29: 11-13 NKJ)

I had my shell, and my mom had her quills. But really, deep inside, we both were just afraid. I was afraid to be anything that would cause me to look better than her. I was afraid to do something with my life or believe in something more for my life because she would react and remind me where I came from and that I should have died. That I came from a pile of shit and always came out smelling like a rose. That there was something wrong with me because my father never stayed. That there was something wrong with me because I did not drink and swear and smoke and participate in her lifestyle. That there was something wrong with me because I wanted to go to church and worship and know who Jesus was and sing and speak and share His love! That there was something wrong with me because I yearned for peace, for joy, for creativity, and for beauty. That there was something wrong with me because I was different from her in many ways, and that frightened her and confused me as her child.

Now, like the porcupine and the turtle, I realize that the quills and shells I see in people are just fear. The confusion that was in me, was due to the fearful, unsafe environment I grew up in. It was a very dark and lonely place. A place that broke my heart to also see my mother live in. A place so isolated from everyone that no one could touch her, no one could get close to her. But now, if I pull into that isolated place, it is no longer a dark and lonely one. It is just a moment to find refuge. To get grounded when I may get triggered by old fears. It is a time to refuel my faith. And in that place, I think of her often.

Love these pictures of my momma

···4···

Can't We All Get Along?

"We could all learn a lot from crayons: some are sharp, some are pretty, some are dull, while others bright. Some have weird names, but they have all learned to live together in the same box. And broken colors, still color." –Unknown

THE SAME BOX my family was all living in became a suffocating one. The insanity from being raised in a broken home with alcoholism, anger, strife, and over-the-top jealousy; at times, it felt like more than I could bear. To this day, many of the same triggers and strongholds still come into play in my relationships. It makes me yearn more and more each day for heaven. As the old hymn goes, "For when we all get to heaven, what a joyful time that will be. When we all get to heaven, we will sing and dance in jubilee." (7) There will be no more tears, no more strife, no more divorce, no more illness, no more anger or evil intent. We truly will be able to live in that one big, beautiful rainbow box of crayons in the sky! There, we will worship and love and be pretty and bright and sharp and not have to be someone we are not or conform to the people-pleasing ways of the world. The jealousy and hurtful ways of people will be gone, and peace and acceptance will prevail.

Growing up in a predominantly female family taught me a lot. I find I would rather have male friends, as I get along better with men. The women in my family were so hurtful to each other. And yet, God made us to be the ones who are great at relationships. But the irony of that is that we are also best at tearing these relationships apart with our insecurities and jealousies. If we could only unite our female bonding strengths, be supportive and happy for each other, build one another up, and rejoice with our sisters—what a truly wonderful world it would be!

This is a tribute to my mother, God rest her soul, but before I can continue and rejoice in all that I have learned from her life and death, I need to address the insanity I so often experienced and still do bump into with other women. I'm talking about the psychological blows and emotional abuse that came from whatever spirit was present in my family. Is it the "Jezebel" spirit? Let me walk through this, as I truly believe it was and still is present in my family.

People considered to be under the influence of the Jezebel Spirit are cunning and manipulative like Jezebel herself. They are masters at distorting the truth with lies and half-truths. They are very charming and adamant and will leave you helpless! They take credit for things they didn't contribute to. They manipulate people to accomplish their agenda and leave no room for others to express an opinion. They love authority and being in control! If Jezebel spirits are confronted, they will not admit guilt or wrongdoing. Instead, they will skillfully twist the entire situation to make themselves look right and the confronter look like the crazy one! If you do confront them, get ready for them to become your worst enemy! They are vengeful and will stop at nothing to destroy your reputation. They love to continually belittle other people to gain control and devalue them—this improves their position of power! Their goal is to annihilate you. (8)

It seems harsh and I know we have to be careful of labeling others with this spirit, whether female or male. As I said, I keep bumping into it. After educating myself on this spirit, I know when I have been in the presence of it because it sucks the life out of me. It leaves me wiped out and under a spell of worthlessness. It is a bit hard to recognize at first because it is so alluring and manipulative. I question if most people who possess it even know that they do! It is a snake that slithers into your life to poison your system.

As I write this, I have just come off the aftermath of this "bite.". I was lured by a stranger who I thought was becoming a friend. They were requiring too much of my time, and in the lure of trying to become a friend, I gave them too much control over my mind, thoughts, and feelings. I've fallen into this pattern as long as I can remember, and most of the time I attribute this "neediness" to wanting so badly to win the approval of my mother and to have known my father.

That neediness became a constant in my relationships with my sisters. I was the youngest, and I felt like I never measured up to them. They were the smart ones, they were the pretty ones, and I was the ugly duckling! I was not like them. I did not feel like I fit in, and Lord knows I tried. But the fitting in seemed to require such a sacrifice of who I was and who I am. I'm not a conformist. I like my space and time alone to create and have my own thoughts and feelings. Trying to fit in and please people is a toehold for the enemy. It is in our inadequacies of trying to prove ourselves to others that he gets us jumping through hoops and not standing on the solid ground of knowing who we are and "whose" we are in Christ. In our instability, we are vulnerable to his attack and control.

I have decided that not fitting in and not walking in the ways of this world is okay! If I have made a genuine attempt to be a friend, sister, or significant other to someone who has then left my life, they did not belong in my life. I believe that God brings people into our lives for a reason, possibly as a lesson for me or for them. Some come just for a season. When the reason or season ends, it's time to let go. Anyone who does not embrace my presence should then experience my absence. "For am I now seeking the favor of men, or God? Or am I striving to please men? If I were still pleasing men, I would not be a servant of Christ." (Galations 1:10 NKJ)

You cannot take everyone with you!

God gave Noah a vision for the ark he was to build and told him that the floods would come. It took him many years to build his ark, and many people laughed at him for the time and effort and detail and commitment he put into his task. They did not believe or feel the need to invest in this as Noah did. When the floods finally came, God pretty much told Noah, if they did not help build it, they cannot get on your ark. He did this because he knew Noah was a compassionate soul and would invite everyone on the ark, even though that would have caused great issues for the ark.

The people who are not there with you to help build your vision, to build your ark, to invest in your vision and invest in your ark...they will only sink your ark! They will be jealous of you when the storms come, and they will wish they had had the discipline, commitment, and vision that you had. For they choose to live in a manner of the world, to live for today and be that pleaser who keeps up with the world in each moment They choose not to spend time alone, knowing what their God-given purpose and true desires are and their ultimate destiny for this life. They are people who are easily swayed by others, by others' opinions, control, and needs. They do not suffer for their standards. They lower them to fit in, and they want you to do so, as well.

The emptiness that comes after being tossed to the curb when you have spent so much time trying to get someone's approval over and over again brings me to the roots of this

Jezebel spirit. After an encounter with it, I retreat, and then set my standards higher and my boundaries tighter. It is easy to set those boundaries and standards. Not as easy to keep them! We teach people how we want to be treated, how to love us. I have been, in the past, an enabler to the crime of my own mistreatment. The deprivation of love and acceptance I had as a child led me, at times, to a kind of blindness. I chose to not pay attention to red flags that were fiercely waving in front of me. I did know they were there. I just chose to not see them!

"He who winks with an eye, causes trouble." (Prov 10:10 NKJ)

So, in 2019, I am spending another Christmas and birthday alone. Embracing my aloneness. I love spending this day digging deep into my heart and writing. I love hanging out with my animals, which helps me understand the peacefulness of that first Christmas. I recently listened to a fabulous message by one of my favorite speakers, the Bishop T.D. Jakes. It's called "Rejoice in your Rejection." That first Christmas, there was no room for them in the inn. They had gone many miles and knew that the time was coming soon…but they were turned away. Mary was uncomfortable and Joseph was disappointed that this journey was not turning out as he thought it would. It was hard to keep going. The world was watching and not believing them. None of this made any sense!

The rejection became God's redirection to a humble stable where animals could welcome them, the sheep could guard them, and a star—God's only light! —shone above. All these things had to be present for the rejected couple to feel safe, for they must have felt abandoned at that point. Really, is a King not to be born in a nice hotel room with room service and all the pampering and care one would expect? But God knew what He was doing when He allowed the redirection from the inn. He had already instructed the wise men and their camels to follow the star and that they would find a manger. If Mary and Joseph had been able to stay in the inn, they would have missed the wise men; they would have missed the frankincense, gold, and myrrh.

It is amazing how many times my attempt to fit in, to abandon myself and be controlled by the Jezebel spirits in my life have distracted me from the gifts of frankincense, gold, and myrrh that were coming to me. Too often, I found myself as the little girl who so desperately wanted the approval of my mother, my stepfather, and my sisters, constantly knocking on their door to let me in—please, let me in! I cannot bear to be out in the cold, out in the barn. There just never seemed to be room for me. As a little girl, I made my room in an unfinished attic, alone, vowing to never ask anything from anyone again!

And yet, after 50 some years of being pushed out of people's lives and rejected because I did not believe or act the way they did, I find that my most peaceful place to be this Christmas, is the barn. My little dog and two horses love me unconditionally and protect me more than anything, for they choose me. I do not have to force their love or need to put them on a leash or lead rope. The love, commitment, care, and consistent acceptance and understanding I have given them, comes back to me in a love that is indescribable. Why can't we humans get this?

I have given that same kind of love, kindness, and care to many in my life, especially to my mother. For many years, I tried to be pleasing and sensitive to her. I exhausted myself trying to figure out the cause of her Jekyll and Hyde personality, trying to figure out how I could have helped her and how I could have been more accepting of her. I would pour myself into her over and over again. I would also do this with many friendships and relationships, only to get zapped at the end for never being enough!

My mother's death has helped free me of a lot of this, but I still bump into that spirit out there. As I said, after every bump, I slow down, get realigned, and try once again to proceed with caution into relationships. I try not to be blind to the red flags or dismiss the controlling, manipulative spirits, or put so much into taking care of someone that I lose my balance and stop taking care of me and my dreams and desires that God has put in my heart.

Heed this! It is not a selfish thing to practice self-care. If a plane is going down, you are not of any help to anyone else if you do not put that oxygen mask on yourself first. Unfortunately, the unhealthy people in my life see my self-care as selfish. I think it is their lack of understanding what self-care means. I also see that people who do not practice having boundaries and setting limits for themselves want others to continue to jump through hoops for them and be a part of their toxic behaviors.

I hope and pray that my efforts and intentions in my recovery and quest for a healthy life will help to break the generational curses in my family—the curses of alcoholism, abandonment, abuse, divorce, and toxic relationships. I would give anything for these generational curses to be changed into generational promises of sobriety, peace, and lifetime commitments to marriage and parenthood. I have made mistakes as a daughter, sister, parent, and spouse, but I pray that those behind me who suffered because of my mistakes will learn and grow from them. Our history in the world, in our country, and in our own lives is there for us to learn and evolve from, not necessarily for us to repeat!

I tried to learn from my mother's and father's mistakes, but any success I had only brought envy from my mother. I did not have the same standards and wishes for my life and family as she had for hers, and she thought that meant that I saw her as a failure. This was not a rejection on my part, only an evolution—to take from her the things that fit for me and let the rest go. This, of course, took a lot of detaching from the family dysfunction and my codependent traits.

I continue to practice my self-care and protect that part of me that is untouchable by others. It is my God time, prayer time, creative time, writing and reading time. These are the things in my life that are inner events and not subject to other people's influence. There is a private joy that comes from this. I have found that many people, including myself, flourish in these moments if you can be disciplined enough to guard and protect these inward gifts that God has given you. Your time, talents, and treasures are God's greatest gift to you. Becoming all you are called to be, is your gift back to Him.

"Your gift will make room for you." (Prov 18:16 NKJ)

Broken crayons, still color---

As a little girl, I spent hours in that little unfinished attic I called my room, making dresses for my dolls from scraps of fabric from the dresses my mother had made for me. Sewing was an art that was passed down in my family, and I embraced it with all my spirit. So, at the age of seven, I made my first pair of low-rise bell bottoms. They were a big trend back then. The first pair I made were of a big, bold plaid. No one had anything like them, and it sparked in me how I could do something unique and have my own sense of style and not have to be like my sisters or my girlfriends. There was envy from others in this, but their envy fueled me. I knew it was my frankincense, gold, and myrrh. It was my gift.

Broken crayons,
still color---

I made my own clothes because I hated having to wear my sisters' hand-me-downs. I also did it because I felt rejected by my mother; at this point in her life, she was always too busy to sew clothes for me as she had when I was little. So, I decided to learn to do this myself. Over the years, I have created and made some magnificent clothes, gowns, and costumes. I love those Cinderella moments and am grateful now for the gift of rejection that fueled my talent to create!

I never thanked my mother for that, and I wish I had. So, I pause now and say a prayer and offer that up to her with gratitude. When I sew, I no longer feel the bitterness that once was there for feeling rejected or feeling like I did not fit in with the other girls because I had handmade clothes. There was a divine redirection in that.

Sewing is truly a dying art and one I hope to pass on to my granddaughters. It seems amazing today that my true talents were, at one time, gifts that my mother had instilled in me. Sewing, writing, reading, gardening, cooking, and animals. They all came from her initially. And after many years of not wanting to be like her in any way, ---I have embraced all that she has taught me! I have the patience of Job when it comes to piecing together beautiful creations of fabric, yarns, beads, and threads. Why could I not have had that same patience for her? For other difficult people in my life? I could have been nicer to my mother. I could have been there for her a lot more than I was. I was just too wounded and hurt to allow myself to feel vulnerable in her presence. I allowed my mother's wounds and her hurtful words towards me to define me.

Never did I think that my heart would be where it is today. It is Christmas time, and all I want to do is give, help others, and make the world a safer, more lovely place. It all began in a barn, with the star and the animals. Look up and see the guiding light. Make your world a safer place for other people to be in or not be in. Accept them as they are. Do not get hurt when there is no room in the inn. It is a divine redirection! The camels are coming, and they are carrying the gifts of frankincense, gold, and myrrh.

Wait for it and claim it.

Hold on to your joy.

Hold on to His promise!

My Cinderella moments

···5···

Her Softer Side

"Sit with animals quietly and
they will show you their hearts.
Sit with them kindly and they
will help you find yours...." (9)

EVERY DAY, I am reminded of my mom's softer side as I look
into the big brown eyes of her little Shih Tzu, Buddy. I found
him at a shelter and wanted so desperately to get him for her. I
realized that she was spiraling down a bit and needed a purpose
to get up every morning, since her last little dog had passed a
couple of years ago. I, being an animal lover as well, knew that
if she had a furry friend that she could care for and cuddle with,
and help get her out for a walk here and there, she would soften
a bit and her heart would be more approachable. So, Buddy came
to live with her at Christmas in 2014. He is a rescue dog and has
abandonment issues of being left in a kennel and no one coming
back for him. Mom and Buddy instantly bonded.

I got to witness her bonding with someone a few times over the course of her life, always with her animals, her grandsons, and her father, my grandfather. I would get somewhat jealous, as I wish she could have had that bond with me. She and I did have a bond, but it never lasted long. Something always seemed to trigger some drama or conflict in our relationship that would sever any closeness we had. I really hated it!

But I get it. My heart, too, is always softened by my animals, my son, my grandkids, and my Heavenly Father. They bring out the little girl in me that wants to connect to their innocence, their need to be loved and cared for without a lot of issues and grown-up drama. Even though my son is a grown man and we have had our times of disconnect and differences, he is still my little boy in my heart. I love keeping my heart tender towards him. And of course, my Heavenly Father and my alone time with Him brings a peace beyond human understanding.

I loved watching the tenderness that Buddy brought to my mom, and I'm grateful that he brings it to me today with his eagerness to greet me each morning, sitting by my side as I work or read or write, and following me wherever I go throughout my house and yard. He truly is my Buddy! I also loved watching my mom and how loving she was towards her grandsons. They had a very special bond.... much like the bond I had with my own grandfather.

I know I thought my mother was harsh and cold towards me a lot when she was alive because she didn't very often show me her softer side. It made my heart hard and frustrated towards her because of the constant guilt and blame she put on me. I came upon a letter from her recently that somewhat spoke about it.

Kristy,

Thank you for the last letter. Since we last talked, I have had another reaction to yet another medication, so I am not feeling very good.

I was considering coming back, but I am just not up to it.

I have tried to understand what has gone on over the years but being totally rejected by those I love and have loved has finally taken its toll on me.

I won't be a burden or an embarrassment to anyone of you.

I love my grandson very much and will always cherish the times we had together. But I won't ruin his special Graduation Day by causing anyone any anguish or stress by me being there.

It's also hard on me knowing that my presence causes all of that to all of you and for that I am sorry.

I have enjoyed our visits, but I have found I can no longer join in conversations...all I can do is sit and listen and be uncomfortable.

Please get your brother back into your family. He hasn't done anything but support me in whatever I have decided to do...right or wrong. If he has judged me, I've not heard about it.

I have no idea how much longer I'll be around, but I'll make the best of each year I have with or without my family.

In spite of all of this, I love all of you very much, I always have and always will.

I am very proud of all of you, and I know all of your accomplishments were achieved on your own.

I hope you can understand how I feel and have felt all of these years.

I love you too,
Mom

Naturally, this pierced my heart. And yet, there are times I feel that same way around my own grown child. I feel guilty for the things I wish I would have done differently in raising him and the mistakes I made. I feel guilty at how he has had to suffer some of the consequences because of my decisions. Sometimes, it feels like my son won't forgive me for my mistakes, that he feels like I should have done better. Then, I remember how my mother reacted when I decided to raise my own child differently than she had done. I think it is just the way the next generation starts to act as their parents get older; the grown children become wiser and advanced in their own raising of children. That to us older parents can feel like rejection, but we are wise with understanding if we choose not to lash out.

Could we all have done it better? Perhaps, but, many of us did not know how to do something different than how we were raised. Sometimes, it takes the pain of hurtful decisions and the aftermath of that pain to push you forward and help the next generation do something different. It's easy to pridefully believe that our children will turn out better off because we won't make the same mistakes our parents did. Do we really believe this? I know I did.

Parents do the best for their children with what they know at the time. Everything is a process and a learning experience. Children do not come with a manual.

My heart is grateful now, thinking about the joy my mother had with these special people and animals in her life. There is healing in me in this moment, realizing that those relationships for her were so pure and unconditional and that her soul needed them and responded to them.

I do not know if I will ever understand her relationship with my grandfather. She would comment at times, that she experienced physical abuse from him. Perhaps her need for that love and approval of the opposite sex parent set the tone for how I saw her relate to him. My grandmother died when I was four years old, and I do not remember her. Maybe the tenderness my mother had towards my grandfather was the result of many years she saw him care for my grandmother as she lay bedridden in their apartment, dying of cancer.

My grandparents had a small-town mom and pop restaurant. They were fabulous cooks, making everything from scratch. My first job was bussing tables and doing dishes at the age of five at their restaurant. They were closed on Sundays, so after my grandmother died, my grandpa would come to our house for Sunday dinner. It by far was my favorite childhood memory. I **loved** my grandpa!! He brought joy to our house. He had such a jolly spirit, and he used to write me the most creative letters. Granted, he would have had a few beers before he penned them, but I loved receiving them.

He was a Johnny Cash fan and would often write letters that included song lyrics. Once, he wrote that he was sitting in the back of the restaurant, listening to "Five Feet High and Rising" on the radio, when suddenly the table started to move and soon, he was being lifted by a current of water that was filling the whole place. He was not sure if he should continue to write to me, to grab his beer or to start swimming for help. I don't remember the rest of the story—how he creatively made it to shore—but I will never forget how much I loved getting his letters and how they made me laugh.

What a contrast! As a little girl, loving and desperately wanting to be in the presence of my grandpa and hanging on to every word he wrote to me as I so loved his jolliness, his wit, and his creativity. Compare that to the dread, fear, and relentless pain I experienced with the letters and presence of my own mother.

With that, I choose to forgive my mother and remember the joy she gave to her grandsons as my grandfather gave to me.

"Honor your father and your mother, so that you may live long in the land the Lord your God is giving you." (Exodus 20:12 NKJ)

This is the first earthly relationship addressed in the commandments, and it is the only one to come with a blessing from God.

As defined by Bible Study Tools, to honor someone is to give weight or grant a person of position respect and even authority in one's life. To prize highly, care for, show respect, and obey. (10)

I honor them. I look to those who have gone before me and did the best they knew to do. Believers or not, it is part of God's eternal plan that we obey and honor our parents, that we choose to see the best in them, even after their time in this life ends. I honor their memory and all that they were.

I honor them by choosing to forgive. I know I will fall short of this at times, but I am reminded that we all make mistakes. We need to trust that the Lord has placed us in the care of those before us for a reason, and that He does not make mistakes.

I honor them by releasing judgment for their behavior to a just God who has protected me and shown me tremendous mercy and compassion!

I honor them for His word tells me that He will bless me for doing so.

I honor and bless the generations that have gone before me and the legacies and lessons they have left for me to learn.

I honor them as I work to clear my generational trauma. I must not forget to claim the generational strengths. My ancestors gave me more than just wounds.

Grandma, Mom, and me…1964

Grandma and Grandpa

Grandpa, the chef of his café

Mom and her grandsons

Grandma is so proud of you, JR.

Mom, being a proud grandma...2004

And she would be a very proud great grandma!

···6···

Her Illness

"Though I walk in the midst of trouble you will revive me. You will stretch out your hand against the wrath of my enemies and your right hand will save me." (PS 138:7 NKJ)

Hi Mom,
Happy Birthday!!   **March 2018**

March is a crazy weather month for us Midwesterners, so I have come to Florida to get out of the cold and see the sunshine and palm trees. Thought it would help my spirits a bit and get the "winter of my soul" thawed out.

It was always so hard for me to think of you living alone in rural Nebraska during the winter months, as I worried so much about you being safe and warm and being able to get to a nearby town for groceries and your basic needs. That last year you were alive was the hardest. I knew your mind and health were failing. I hated being so far away from you. I had promised my sister that I would back off from intervening in helping you and let her handle it.

Her contacting an agency and having a nurse come out and evaluate you and your living conditions was an awful experience for you, and for that I am sorry. You had been such an independent woman your whole life. I cannot imagine the defenses that came over you during that time, not to mention the fear of what was happening. I wish I had been there for you. It is only in hindsight that I see the domino effect of this, of the initial seeds of stripping you of your independence. None of us even want to imagine when we reach that stage in our lives, yet many take this so lightly when the time comes for us to do it to others.

Why did I resort to thinking that my sister "knew best?" Just because she is the oldest and had lots of experience with government agencies and connections. I feel she completely missed what mattered most: your heart, your mind, your spirit. She sent an agency out and they came and did their short evaluation and sent her their report. The report said you had early signs of dementia. A diagnosis that I think is very readily diagnosed these days.

It probably was not a good choice to just send you a letter with this diagnosis in it. No one was there with you to hold your hand or tell you they would be there to help you and take care of you, No one was there to calm you, to pray with you, to talk through what this all meant for you and your future and your living conditions. It was very insensitive to drop this to you in the mail! As I look back, I can see how your health spiraled as a result of it. I saw what happened when they labeled you and told you something was wrong with you. It really created a blast of mine fields to go off in you!

You reacted as you had in the past: writing letters to express your feelings to me. They were up and down; verbally abusive and accusing! I had again become your scapegoat, and it all was very ugly. I knew I would have to go up against the force of my sister if I chose to express my disagreement in how she wanted to handle your situation, and I knew your reaction was not going to be one I wanted to endure either. I then resorted to my turtle shell and chose to take the attack of your quills versus hers! I knew something had to be done to intervene in your life, but I also knew there were other ways to do it, ways that would have been more loving.

My remorse now doesn't change anything for you, but I do need to say it because that is what my heart feels. I wish I had stood up for you. I wish I had gotten the report and taken it out to you and helped you walk through the difficult news and uncertainty. My feelings of remorse now are to help bridge the gap of this character defect of mine. "I am sorry" means that I want a heart change, as I don't want to be like that anymore. I do not want to live in that passive, avoiding, victim behavior. It is not easy to change after a lifetime of this. It was a crazy upbringing, Mom! I am not saying that to you to cut you down or hurt you or tell you anything you do not already know. You passed down all that you knew, and I then developed my own skills to cope with all the chaos and dysfunction.

What do I do now? Does writing this story help? It doesn't help you, but it is helping me and, hopefully, the next generation or someone reading this who can learn from it. Isn't that why God allows us to go through these experiences? To help others, to comfort others. And, in turn, to help us grow and comfort us?

Sitting now at a keyboard and writing (or should I say bleeding?) out all of this is supposed to bring me comfort. Really? It hurts! It is emotionally exhausting to relive. It would be much easier to avoid this piercing sword in my chest. However, the whole experience was so life-changing that my soul yearns to dislodge the sword and heal. So, let me just put it out there:

You were not the cleaned-up, Christian mother I wanted you to be, the June Cleaver mother that my friends seemed to have. I was ashamed of your drinking, ashamed of your vulgar mouth and smoking. I was ashamed of the nights when you were not at home but had stopped at the bowling alley or corner bar and I would come to find you playing pool and wrestling with men. Literally on the ground, wrestling! You were a "tough broad," as you often described yourself. I could not relate to any of this. I wanted your tender side, your feminine side. I wanted your peaceful, sober side.

Your hard-hearted side I know I have in me, as well, though I have tried to deny it over the years. The times I have let it out were followed by deep remorse and shame. I never wanted that side of you. I hated and despised it. Especially when it was unleashed on me! I often feared that I would become like the out-of-control machine that you were. I told my therapist of this fear many years ago. He shared a quote from C.S. Lewis with me that I have tucked deep in my heart.

"If you are a poor creature—poisoned by a wretched up-bringing in some house full of vulgar jealousies and senseless quarrels—saddled, by no choice of your own, with some loathsome sexual perversion—nagged day in and day out by an inferiority complex that makes you snap at your best friends—do not despair. He knows all about it. You are one of the poor whom He blessed. He knows what a wretched machine you are trying to drive. Keep on. Do what you can. One day (perhaps in another world, but perhaps far sooner than that) He will fling it on the scrapheap and give you a new one. And then you may astonish us all—not least yourself: for you have learned your driving in a hard school." C. S. Lewis (11)

• • •

"Teach us to number our days, that we may present to you a heart of wisdom." PS 90:12 (NKJ)

I was on the road in May of 2015 and was listening to a podcast with James McDonald as he preached a sermon on this verse. I had been in a bit of depression for several months and feeling the passive pain of not giving myself a voice in standing up for you. I was driving and really hoping for the end to come, for my life to hurry along and for the good Lord to take me home. As I was listening to this message, He spoke very directly, "So if you live to be 70, how many more years does that give you—15 to 20?" At the time, I was 53, and I thought WOW! I had never visualized it like that—that I could possibly only have another 15-20 years to live. That does not seem like much time at all. What in the world am I doing with my life? Why am I so downcast? Why am I so mindlessly wandering, being passive in my relationship with you and the dreams I have always wanted to pursue—horses, writing, traveling. His message continued with a harsh reality: "What if I died tomorrow?"

At that moment, I felt a jolt in my spirit and a jolt in my body, as I was slammed into from behind on the interstate. I was traveling through a construction zone and had slowed down as the lanes were curving and merging. There were huge concrete dividers in the middle of the road, and I had just passed them when I was struck. The impact threw me into oncoming traffic! I remember seeing a large orange semi-truck coming straight for me. I took my hand off the wheel, closed my eyes, and, in an out-of-body moment, yelled, "I'm dead!"

When my car came to a complete halt, I opened my eyes, in shock that I was alive. I managed to get out of my car only to realize that I was on the far side of the interstate with major traffic passing by me. My car was heading down the bank. The car that hit me was still out in the middle of the construction zone.

Several cars had witnessed the accident. They had stopped and were all gathered out by the other car. The other driver, along with other witnesses, cautiously made their way across the three lanes of congested traffic to help me. A witness put his arm around me and asked if I was okay. I was not sure. He sweetly said that I obviously had a guardian angel watching over me, as my car had swerved through three lanes of oncoming traffic, and nothing hit me. He said it was amazing to watch! All I remember was taking my hand off the wheel.

"Jesus take the wheel, take it from my hands. I can't do this on my own, I'm letting go! Give me one more chance and save me from this road I'm on!!" (12)

The whole ordeal shakes me up even today as I write about it. I remember the profoundness of the message I was listening to and the state of mind I was in, how my heart ached to be living more intentionally in my relationship with you, with my son, and with the people closest to me. I needed that jolt.

This set me back a couple of weeks, dealing with the logistics of it all and the emotional trauma. I had promised to come up and see you a couple weeks from the time of the accident. You needed to pick up your new glasses so you could get your driver's licenses renewed. I knew you were living in a lot of anxiety and fear because your eyes were failing, and your license had expired. You had called me, hysterical, describing the danger that you had been in driving home from your eye doctor appointment, your eyes still dilated, unable to see the road. I wanted to help you, but now I did not have a car and was overwhelmed with my own situation. I called my ex-husband and he graciously agreed to drive you to get your new glasses. He thanked me for the time you two spent together that day, as you both always enjoyed each other's company and had some catching up to do. I was grateful.

My sister agreed she was going to see you and make sure you were doing okay. She did, and then I received another awful letter from you. Actually, over the course of a few weeks, I received several of these letters from you. It seemed that whenever my sister connected with you, it triggered your anger and fear! Your letters were once again your outlet. My turtle shell kicked in, but I can't say that I didn't do anything—I prayed and prayed and prayed!

My sister called me to tell me that she had visited you and what she had observed. She was angry with you. She lashed out about how you were not taking care of yourself, you were not eating, you did not care. You just did not care.

As I listened to her angry words about how you were not eating, a little voice inside of me said, "It's not that she is not eating. Something is eating her."

It was only a matter of time before that truth would prevail.

I had not seen you since January, which had been a wonderful visit with you. I had been excited to come and see you, as I was anxious to see you with Buddy. It was awesome to see how you and Buddy had bonded since bringing him home at Christmas. He had given you a purpose to get up every morning. To have something other than yourself to care for. I loved watching the two of you together.

Now, it was five months later. I had been working in Sioux City that day and took that peaceful country drive out to rural Nebraska to see you. It was a surprise visit because I was afraid that if I told you I was coming, you would find some excuse not to see me. I really wanted to see for myself what was happening to you.

There are no words to describe the shock I experienced when you came to the door! My heart sank—you were a ghost. Eyes sunken, and fragile as a twig, hanging on to whatever limb of life you had left in you. It was hard for me to focus and not be so distracted by your drastic change in appearance. Your hands shook with every move you made. I, of course, wanted to be the caretaker and just get you food or doctors or help or something. You kept saying that this was just a bug and that if the weather would straighten out, you would get over it. We made a list of food that you thought would be easy for you to make and that you would hopefully have an appetite for. I then proceeded to the grocery store.

I go numb remembering this night. I didn't know what to feel, what to do, or what to say. Again, I prayed, and I prayed, and I prayed.

I came back and tidied up your house and put the groceries away. I had come not only to see you and find out what was going on with you physically and emotionally, but also to have a conversation with you that I had been afraid to have for several years. I had never talked to you about my faith, about my belief that you must accept Jesus in your heart if you are going to live with him in eternity.

We never went to church together as a family or prayed together or talked much about God or any of this at all. When I went to college, I was introduced to a Baptist church by a dear friend. I had never been exposed to this type of faith. Some of it seems a bit judgmental to me now. But at the time, I really absorbed all of it, as I was very hungry for a foundation and to be grounded in a faith. I realize now that my image of myself as a Baptist helped protect me from the vulgarity, the unrighteousness, the sexual abuse, and the drunkenness of my family. I needed this to help clean me up and take away my shame. Naturally, I did not think that you were saved, that you believed you had Jesus in our heart. You were the wretched sinner; I was the righteous, born-again believer who was always going to save you.

I was on a mission that night, but not just to really see how you were doing. My pride and self-righteousness were on a mission to examine your heart. I was much like the agency nurse who came out to examine you. I was there to determine if I thought you would be spending eternity with Jesus.

I don't remember how the conversation began or even much of what we said. I know you had some intense moments of giving me the evil eye, and I swore I was not backing down from the fear I felt. I was going to tell you what I thought and believed and somehow, we were going to have this difficult conversation. Time was not on your side and, after years of praying for you, I could not bear the thought of not knowing if I would ever see you again in heaven!

I sat on the floor beside you and asked you, "If you died tomorrow, would you go to heaven?" You replied, "That depends on if Jesus will have me. It's up to Him." My heart understood your answer. Many of us think we are not good enough, and I think many of us question to some degree if He really is going to let us in.

I am grateful to have read and listened to many preachers who have taught me 1 John 5: 11-13. "And this is the testimony: God has given us eternal life, and this life is in His son. Whoever has the son has life; whoever does not have the son of God does not have life. I write these things to you who believe in the name of the son of God so that you may KNOW that you have eternal life."

I was ready to unleash my scripture memory on you, so that you would KNOW that you have eternal life. I have seen many well-meaning Christians do this. They quote scripture with their heads and miss meeting people where they are and hearing with their hearts. The Holy Spirit stopped me. Instead, I listened. You began to tell me that you had accepted Jesus in your heart many years ago and that you prayed to Him every night—whether I believed it or not.

I was speechless.

I was not floored by the news that you had accepted Him in your heart years ago, or that you prayed every night. I was speechless when you very firmly, with a bit of boldness and anger in your voice, said, "Whether you believe it or not." It was probably one of the most humbling moments of my life. Who am I? What have I done to think that other people need to prove their faith and their prayers and their relationship with Jesus to me? When and where along my faith journey did, I elevate myself to such a standard that I think others, especially my own mother, has to prove this to me?

"The Lord does not see as man sees; for man looks at the outward appearance, but the Lord looks at the heart." (1 Sam 16:7 NKJ)

This had been an underlying current in our relationship for a long time. I had judged your outward addictions and behavior and never once had asked you if you believed. I just assumed that you did not! I assumed that, since you did not clean yourself up and go to church like I did, and because you drank and swore and smoked and I did not, then you certainly were not a Christian.

As I knelt beside your trembling, fragile little self, reached out and grabbed your hands. With the humblest of repenting tears, I poured my heart out to you for forgiveness for the years I had judged you. The years I had wrongly thought of myself so much better than you because of my "cleaned-up Christian faith." I was anything but Christ-like during those years. I just hid behind my faith. I was ashamed of you, and I needed something to take away that shame. In my heart, I knew Jesus took my shame away, but I had never forgiven you for the shame that you caused.

I had always envisioned a moment like that night, but in my imagination, it was you asking for my forgiveness. I truly, until then, did not know that I needed yours! I was in such denial of my self-righteousness and the gap that caused in our relationship. I had focused for so many years on the pain and hurt that you had caused me and had never once realized the pain I caused you by being so ashamed of you. You were not my ideal mother. You were not like my friends' mothers. And for that, now, I am grateful. You were you. You did not care what people thought of you. If you had something to say, you were going to say it. You broke every mold and refused to conform. Almost to a fault, you rebelled and went so far the other way. I did not know how to find a balance, so I also rebelled—and went to the other extreme!

I was 53 years old and had been a born-again believer for over 30 years. I had been on mission trips and prayed with many a stranger in a foreign land and now, for the first time in my life, I had the courage to pray with my own mother. What was I so afraid of? I told myself I was afraid you would reject me and think that my wanting to pray with you would just be some "holier than thou" moment. I did not want you to ridicule my faith or cut me down for it. I also did not want you to say anything negative about Jesus the way you always did about my real father. That is what I told myself. But now, I think I just didn't want to be vulnerable with you. Being vulnerable and praying with you would have been a form of intimacy, and I really didn't want to be that close. I had been hurt too many times in trying to get close to you. My relationship with Jesus was and is my personal relationship, and I was not going to allow you to touch it!

I left that night and told you I would call every day and make sure you were eating and doing okay. I told you that if you did not get better soon, I would come back and take you to the doctor. You agreed.

Oh, the tears, way too many to count were shed from both of us that night.

I drove to my hotel, 30 minutes away, with tears streaming endlessly! The radio was playing as I drove in a daze about what had just taken place. The Plumb song "Lord, I'm Ready Now" started to play. The words poured over my heavy heart.

"I just let go, and I feel exposed. But it's so beautiful, 'cause this is who I am. I've been such a mess, but now I can't care less. I could bleed to death…I was so caught up, in who I'm not. Can you please forgive me? I've nothing left to hide, no reasons left to lie. Give me another chance. Lord, I'm ready now!" PLUMB (13)

I cried like a baby all night, thinking of the wasted years of unforgiveness and judgment towards you that I had been carrying, and how that had kept me so far away from someone

I claimed to love so much. I had been told by a therapist years ago that to heal from the wounds of you, I needed to embrace how we were similar and not focus on our differences. I never could embrace that. I always had to have the defense that I was nothing like you. There was too much shame to embrace you.

Now the walls were down. Time was running out, and I wanted to make this count. Please forgive me.

I cried and prayed all night.

Mom, this letter has taken me several days to write. I have been wanting to share with you in writing so much of all these memories and feelings. I hope they never fade from me. I hope they live on for whatever healing purpose they may need to.

It is now Easter morning. I love Easter. I love spring and the re-birth of the earth! The trees and the flowers. I remember one Easter when I was a little girl and you had made me a new dress and coat. It was yellow and white pique, much like the simple little dresses and coats that Jackie O. had made famous in the 1960s. I loved getting new clothes, especially the ones you made me. I loved dressing up and going to church, even if it meant going alone when I was little. I ran out the door that morning, so excited about my new dress and the promise of spring. The sun was finally out after several days of rain and mud. In my excitement, I ran out the door and down the early morning dewy hill and completely wiped out in the mud! My new dress and coat were totally soiled. I was devastated.

For is not that what Easter is all about? Jesus came to wash us clean. For we are all as dirty, filthy rags in need of a Savior and His cleansing blood. I have spent a lifetime putting on my pretty new dresses and heading off to church. Perhaps I was thinking that is what will make me okay, will make me feel accepted and clean and different from you. Make me more Christ-like, more Christian, more saved.

How humbling.

"Come out of sadness from wherever you've been. Come broken hearted, let rescue begin. Come find your mercy, oh sinner come kneel. Earth has no sorrow, that heaven can't heal. Lay down your burdens and lay down your shame, all who are broken, come as you are." Crowder (14)

Happy Easter, Mom!

He has risen. He has risen indeed!

Love you,
Kristy

···7···

Her Final Days

Mary, did you know, that this child you delivered...
would soon deliver you?

Dear Mom, 8-1-18

It is coming up on the third anniversary of your death.
This week is bittersweet. My heart is full because I remember the fabulous moments, I had sitting by your side every day,
watching your every breath. I prayed and held your hand and
felt such peace about where this journey had led us. I never
thought it would end the way it did—so suddenly and so
life-changing to be tossed in the whirlwind of it all.

As I look back, the responsibility to step up and help make
so many health and end of life decisions for you and trust that
what I felt was the right thing, was all that I wanted. It was all
that mattered. No matter how much I had blown opportunities to be the daughter I could have been to you, this was it!
And I believed that you, more than anyone, had the right to

die and live out your life in dignity, surrounded by the people who would love on you and care for you. I knew if you would just surrender your strong will of wanting to be alone and be independent and care for yourself, that you would soften. That you would find some solace in allowing others to do for you what you could no longer do for yourself. I had wanted this for you for so long.

I have two of the most vivid memories of those final days. I had come back home for a few days and was quite miserable. People at work told me to just go back and be by your side. So, I packed up and drove that long drive up to Minnesota. It was after 8 pm when I arrived, and I was afraid that the nursing home would not let me visit you that late. I snuck in and saw a nurse from a distance and asked if I could please just go spend a few minutes with you. She agreed.

I was tired, and you were as well. I sat by your bedside and held your hands, the same hands that held me as a child. I was now holding on to yours for dear life. Oh, I did not want to let go. I had just found you again. The mother I knew as a child with a tender heart and a fiery spirit. The mother who recognized that I, her baby, was tired of being so strong for her as she was wasting away. I began to cry, and the tears were like fresh rain to my soul. You reached for me and asked, "Why are you crying?"

I responded, "I'm not ready to say goodbye."

With that, you reached out to me like I was your little girl, not in wanting anything from me, but to give me something so precious that I, as a 53-year-old woman, had no idea I needed. I needed your arms and hands to hold me one last time. To let me lay my head on your shoulder and cry like a baby because I was losing my mom. Your baby girl, wishing for life to stand still and bottle this precious moment because I didn't want it or you to go away!

Oh, I was tired, so tired, from years of being so strong for you and for me. You were tired, tired of the battles in your own life and the fear of letting yourself love like you had never been hurt before. You showed me pure, unconditional love as a mother does for her child—one last time. And for that I am eternally grateful. I knew you were passing the baton to me. To be the mother and grandmother you had desperately tried to be, with all your demons and pain. But before taking hold of that baton, I got to be your little girl one last time. To be sad, to be weak, to be held and loved by her mamma!

You held me for the longest time and just let me cry. Patting and rubbing my back as if to say, *"It is all going to be okay. Let it out…I know the grief and pain you are feeling. I, too, walked my mother through her dark season of cancer and death. I, too, had to be strong for my mother and care for her to the end with all her demons and illness."*

Your tenderness seemed one of gratitude for being there for you. Your frail body, with all its strength, just laid there and held me and let me weep. Wiping my tears and saying nothing. It was the most touching moment of my life. It felt like we were reliving the memory of the Christmas Eve when I was lying on your lap and staring up at the stars and listening to you sing so sweetly "Silent Night, Holy Night."

"It was a holy night, all was calm, all was bright, mother and child, love's pure light, sleep in heavenly peace, sleep in heavenly peace." (15)

No words were really spoken. We held each other and I cried for over an hour, until we both fell into a peaceful sleep.

"Occasionally, in life, there are those moments of unutterable fulfillment which cannot be completely explained by those symbols called words. Their meanings can only be articulated by the inaudible language of the heart." (16) MLKJ

I spent the next several days coming to see you with Buddy. You so loved that little dog, and he loved coming to your room and hopping up on your bed and loving all over you. The nurses and staff loved him, and he was in his prime, being so adored by everyone. One day, Buddy jumped up on your bed into your lap, and you let out a loud painful squeal and snapped, "Kristy, there is a dog in here...get him out." I thought you were just joking and told you it was just Buddy. "Remember, Mom? Your dog, Buddy?"

To that, you replied, "I don't have a dog."

I knew things were changing quickly then. The one thing you had loved so dearly and wanted to have near you until the day you died was Buddy. I had fought like heck to make sure that wish was granted, but your mind was now pretty gone. The cancer had spread from your lungs and spine to your brain. It was beyond painful to watch. The nurses could not keep up with the morphine to keep you comfortable. It was impossible for you to lie too long without being in horrible pain, and you would scream for help to move you or to pee or to give you some relief. Your eyes were dark and hollow, your lips a dry pale white, and every breath lingered like it was going to be your last.

I wrote your obituary, remembering the conversations we had had when I was driving you to the ER and reminiscing about your childhood, your parents, and your life. You had such a vivid memory of all of that, even though most days, you couldn't remember if you had had lunch. I wanted to hear those stories one more time. Many of the details I had forgotten or had never really comprehended, as I did not see the importance. Now I realized it was your life, your legacy, and it mattered. It mattered to me, to your grandsons, and would matter to your great-grandchildren—and on and on!

As I wrote, you were resting peacefully; they had increased your morphine. Suddenly, you looked up with the most radiant and focused eyes. You lifted your right hand as if you were reaching for someone. I froze and watched in awe. There was an aura of light around your face. You saw something, someone, and it was pulling you as you continued to reach for it. You had been too frail for days to lift your little body, but something was drawing you, calling for you. I knew it was the Lord's hand reaching for you, and the radiance around your eyes and face were the glimpses of eternity you were seeing.

I have never had such a "God" moment in my life. I was mesmerized by it. Talking about it or sharing it almost seems to diminish the holiness of it. It was breath-taking and such a validation of where you are today. I had prayed and prayed for a sign that the good Lord had you in the palm of His hands. Now, I know without a doubt that your soul is resting in His green pastures.

I spent hours that day holding your hand and rubbing your temples, arms, and shoulders, playing meditation music to keep you calm. I watched over every move, every breath, every flicker of your eyes, and memorized every line and curve on your face. It's how I wanted to remember you: peacefully resting.

I took a break and left for dinner. I came back to your peaceful room, where the curtains had been drawn and the evening lights were casting restful shadows on you. I did not speak. I just sat and prayed, asking the Lord to take you home. To not let you suffer any longer and to let me be there with you when you left this earth. I was determined to stay until the end, whatever that looked like.

I knew my sister was planning on coming to visit the next day, and I knew it would be tense between us. She had not been there since she brought you there six weeks ago. I was processing the whole scenario in my mind and started to get anxious about it, as these last few days with you had been some of the most beautiful moments to me. I did not want anything to take from this incredible peace I had.

With that, you awoke and said very plainly, "Kristy, when is your sister coming back?" You had not spoken so clearly for several days. I knew you asked that for a reason; you were holding on to see her. We had all been there and had our last moments with you. All but my sister.

I replied, "She is coming tomorrow, Mom."

You closed your eyes, said, "Okay," and went back to your peaceful rest.

I sat in silence. It was a message God was giving to me. It was time for me to leave. I had had my time, my precious time with you, and now it was her time. My being there would have only caused stress, and that would have not been fair to anyone. You needed your goodbye with her, and I needed to let go.

The room was dark, the sounds in the halls were silencing, as everyone was turning in. The night nurse was now on duty. I needed to talk to her, as there had been some moments that I was not that kind to her. Moments you were in such pain, I could not bear it, so I snapped at her. She did not deserve it.

She came into your room, and I told her I would be leaving in the morning and my sister was coming. She was surprised, as she did not know I had a sister, which made me feel good. I needed that recognition and validation that I had been there for you, and your daily caretakers knew that I had been. She smiled and said she understood my shortness with her at times, and all was okay.

She left the room, and I went over to sit by your side. I held your hand, caressed your face, put a cold cloth on your brow and lips, and prayed and talked about heaven with you. I talked about the beautiful gardens, the gold streets and the harps and angels that you would soon be seeing. The beautiful house you would be living in and the light, the golden light that would be shining forever around you. That there would be no more darkness, no more pain, or tears, or illness, or anger, or bitterness. It will all be passing away as you enter this glorious place!

With that, you looked at me and said, "Am I going to go live there?"

"Yes Mom," I replied. "You're going to a beautiful place beyond what your eyes or mind can even imagine! All this painful life is going to be over soon. I can't wait to come live there with you!" You nodded and closed your eyes.

"I have to go now, Mom."
"Okay, Kristy Ann, you be careful."
"I will. I love you, Mom."
"I love you, Kristy Ann."

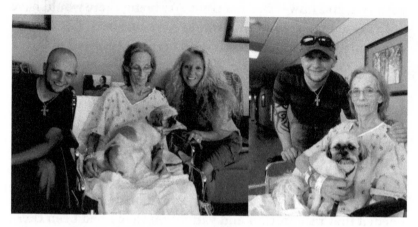

My son, Mom, Buddy, and me

Rest in peace, Mom.

···8···

The Hole In My Heart

I LEFT, KNOWING those were my final words and my last kiss and hug to my mama. It left me numb! It left me wanting the world to stop—wanting to hold on.

The hospice nurse told me that "most people die the way they live." So, it was with my mother. She was very much a loner and loved being away from everyone in her final chapter of life. My sister came to visit the next day. At the end of the day, my son went and said good night to her. It was after everyone had left that she took her last breath—alone.

I was not shocked to hear the news. I found it very comforting to know the fight was now over and she was at peace.

But now what? There was no funeral. My family decided it was not necessary. So, there I was, with this hole in my heart, not knowing how to fill it. I reached out to social media and posted loving photos. I took great pride in writing her obituary and making sure she was honored and acknowledged for her contribution to this earth. I believe we have the right to die with dignity and to be remembered by something that marks our time here. The outpouring of love and condolences from friends on social media was what I needed. I could not just sweep this under the rug and go on like it did not matter or happen. Time needed to stand still for a bit so I could embrace the loss with words, hugs, cards, and tears.

The hardest part followed. For many weeks, I could not stop crying and wishing I had it all to do over. I had found such an incredible purpose in making the end of her life the best it could be, and I loved her like I had never been hurt, like there never had been anything bad between us. It truly was the most intentional I had ever been. Why don't we live like this every day? Why do we wait until the end to make things right? Maybe it is the finality of death that forces us to humble ourselves and see the urgent reality of the situation.

A few times in my life, I have known that I needed to go see someone or reach out to a relative or friend who was sick, and I did not get there in time. I then beat myself up for many months after each occasion. I saw my mother push many people out of her life to protect herself, and I have done the same. There should come a time when connecting to others heals us rather than brings us more pain. Or when we decide the cost of being alone is far more painful than the cost of being present in the lives of people who may not always agree with us or love us like we would like them to.

I still needed closure. Her ashes were sent to the funeral home, and I needed to go back to pick them up and fulfill my promise of scattering them. I returned to Minnesota the following Christmas. On Christmas Eve Day, I went to the funeral home and leaned into this pain again. Funeral homes are quiet, reflective places, and I so needed it that day. I got her box of ashes and asked if I could go to the sanctuary and spend some time alone. "Of course," they replied. "Take as much time as you need."

I sat down and had my own little funeral for my mother. I am a creative soul, so I envisioned what it would have looked like, what songs would have been sung and words would have been spoken in honor of her. I was putting my experiential therapy that I had learned at Onsite many years before into practice again. I then sat and wept and wept and wept. So much of my life with my mother was like this. I had such great visions of how our relationship could have been, how her life could have been, and of course how the end would have been. Not much of my vision came to pass. And for that, I grieved as well.

I was wiped! I left and stopped at the hospital/nursing home where my mother had been. I had a large plate of home-baked cookies that I wanted to take to the nurses., The nurse that I was not always kind to had been a real blessing to my mom. It was hell watching my mom suffer. At times, I, too, was screaming, "Please help her!" My humble apology to that nurse along with my now overwhelming gratitude to her were two very tender moments to me. I knew how hard it was to love my mother and care for her, and this woman was a saint in her caregiving to her.

I had to leave and go meet my son, daughter-in-law, and granddaughter to go to Christmas Eve Mass and spend the evening with them. Things weren't going well with getting a three-year-old ready for church, so I decided to let them work through it. I got in my car with my mom's ashes on the passenger side and we drove around, looking at Christmas lights and sharing many thoughts and feelings, and having a peaceful Christmas Eve together. We had not had many peaceful Christmases in the chaos of our family strife and the pain that Christmas brought us. This was peaceful. She was at peace, and I finally had given up the expectation of this night to be any different, for her to be any different, and for my family to be any different. But life was now different.

A few months passed, and my family had decided to scatter her ashes on the weekend of her birthday. It was a cold March Day, and we met first at the riverbank close to where she grew up. All who wanted to come, came; we each got a cup full of ashes and everyone went and did their own thing with them.

We then drove separately up north to the cemetery where my grandparents were buried. The temps had fallen, and the wind was blustery cold. It was a short moment we spent there, fulfilling her wishes to have her ashes scattered on her parents' grave. Everyone was still in their own state of grief and distance towards each other. Looking back, I realize that was okay. It was a whirlwind of trauma for everyone, and for different reasons. This would take some time to heal.

So, life went on as it does, even though it was slow motion. I would have liked the merry-go-round to stop for a bit so I could get off and take in all the changes that happen in a loss. I found myself, a year and a half later, sitting in the same hospital where my mother breathed her last breath. Now, I was here welcoming a new little granddaughter. I was going to go visit the nursing home where my mother had been so wonderfully taken care of, but I decided it was time to celebrate life! And that is when I felt the healing had really begun. The Lord giveth and the Lord taketh away and blessed be his name.

Now, both of my parents are gone. The baton has been passed for me to now be the one who needs to help make the "grandma" memories. I very much want to do this, though I can only do that as much as my son and daughter-in-law will allow me to. My mother stayed away because she felt it was not "safe" for her to be around her children—we judged her and put her down and made her feel anything but loved most of the time. Not all of that was our fault; she was a difficult person to love and had her own defenses up. I am trying NOT to repeat this. Staying grounded in my faith and my relationship with Jesus Christ is the only answer I have found to overcome getting triggered and jumping through those people-pleasing hoops. When a trigger or rejection occurs, I stop and realize that the only one who can truly fill this connection and love me unconditionally is Christ, and He alone can mend this hole in my heart. My perspective changes. Rather than judging and wanting to prove something to my rejector or get revenge, I step back, lay the situation down at the foot of the cross, and ask Him to take it, to dislodge the piercing sword, the trigger, the pain.

I believe that the hole we all so desperately try to fill will not entirely be filled until we are united with Him in eternity. He puts people in our lives to help us on this journey, to comfort us in our longing for real love. But since He is the one who put this longing in our hearts, it is for Him to fulfill.

It sounds so ideal, does it not? To have people in our lives who are yoked to this belief system. To be healthy enough to recognize that others do not have to meet our needs or approve of us, and that we do not have to approve of them. To have others emotionally available and not live in the fear of disagreement and rejection. To give people the freedom to come in and out of our lives, with no expectation to stay forever. To be a part of our lives for no selfish reason, not to control or manipulate. To honestly hold everyone loosely! To love them unconditionally and rejoice in the lessons and blessings they bring. To allow others to be who and what God made them to be and accept the purpose that we each have in contributing to each other's lives. To not set people up as experts over our lives or exalt ourselves as experts over them, but to save that authority for God. Learn to listen and hear from Him. Let Him tell you what to do. He is your father.

Oh, to love like Christ!

It is a daily process to practice this belief system I have. It is much easier to write and speak about than it is to live. The losses never end. We say goodbye to someone or something every day. My over-processing mind, at first, analyzes the loss to an exhausting point—what could I have done differently to make people stay or to make my presence in their life a better one? It takes a bit of processing, praying, writing, and weeping, and then, I am able to let it go.

Shortly after my mother's death, I often found myself agonizing in my grief, wondering how I could have been different to my mom. Could I have loved her and accepted her more and not been so offended or had this bitterness in my heart towards her drinking and lack of care? Growing up, we didn't have money for our essentials in health care, or new clothes or a new pair of shoes, but there was always money for alcohol and cigarettes. Perhaps, if I had not let her drinking, smoking, and vulgar language make me put up my defenses towards her, I could have had a closer relationship with her. I am grateful to say, I don't get that offended by those issues that much anymore when I see them in other people. A lot of my judgmental attitude has gone away. I think it is because I realize now that I do not have to live with or in that. The daily impact it had on me growing up, I couldn't escape. It defined me too much! I love now that I can choose to separate myself from it.

I notice when I am around vulgar language that my mind picks up on those words and they become a part of my own vocabulary. It then takes a tremendous amount of self-control to not grab those words and use them. I love words—they are such a reflection of our hearts and who we are. I do not want my heart to reflect vulgarity! Now, when I choose not to be around vulgarity, it's not judgment of the other person but simply choosing what I want deposited into my mind and heart.

I have the same feelings about smoking. It was horrible to live in a smoke-filled house. I could not breathe! My eyes burned, and I hated the way my clothes and hair reeked of smoke wherever I went. After I left home, I had the hardest time going back to visit my mother, as I could not handle being around the smoke. When the doctors found her lungs full of cancer, I was not surprised! I was only surprised that she had lived as long as she did; she had been a big smoker since she was in her teens. Most smokers do not realize how selfish that habit is or how it affects others around them who have to live and breathe in it. Watching someone die from it is truly grueling! No doubt that is why I lashed out at her nurse a few times. There were millions of times I wanted to take those cigarettes and burn every one of them. As a child, all I could do was sit and watch it age her quickly and kill her slowly.

I have had such a prejudice against drinking, as well. I have not had a drink in years, but it does not feel like a prejudice anymore. I have struggled with this so much since my mother's death. I am not better or holier than anyone because I do not drink alcohol. Alcohol has never gone well with my system. I have high anxiety, and when that anxiety crashes, it turns into depression. I have learned that I need to stay away from anything mood-altering that will heighten my anxiety. I also truly do believe, there are certain personalities that cannot control these areas of their lives. The enemy can use alcohol and drugs as a foothold to get into a soul and possess it. The lies begin, the addiction takes over, and then life becomes a crazy whirlwind for everyone involved! They have allowed something else to take control of them. The Bible warns us to be not drunk with wine but filled with the Holy Spirit.

I also have learned that an addiction stunts your emotional and spiritual growth. Instead of leaning into the pain, problems, or issues, addicts choose to numb their pain with their drug of choice. Alcohol, drugs, sex, porn, relationships, spending, gambling, food, work—the list can go on and on. Pressing through and leaning into the pain is the sober, holistic way to bring about emotional growth and maturity. Without that effort, you stunt your mental, emotional, and spiritual growth. Your spiritual and emotional muscles need resistance to grow. Adversity, pain, and how you respond, is the weight needed to help accomplish that. No pain...no gain.

I have carried the cross of trying to save someone from addiction for many years. After a while, it becomes not even about the actual person; my soul is just hanging on to the pain and loss of the people in my life who I could not help. Those who could not change and break their addictions. The ones I could not save! This was my own God-like pride. Now I realize that the only way I can help others is to bring them to the source that is pouring through me and filling me up. That Higher Power and source for me is Christ and it is His doing.

My soul now yearns to love others like I loved my mom in the end of her life. I was not trying to save her anymore---I was trying to save myself. To love unconditionally, no agenda, no judgment. To be present and intentional, to be humble, to be forgiving and giving radically for the sake of another. Not expecting anything in return.

When my mother died, she wasn't the only one I lost. The ordeal blew my whole family apart! None of it ended like I thought it would. The last time we had a family death, it brought us all closer together. It did anything but that this time. She was the center of the wheel for her children. There were many needs that were left unmet because of the mother she was or was not. We all grieve differently. We all had our own visions of what the end should have or could have looked like.

Four years later, some of us are just beginning to speak to each other again. We never speak of her or the issue of her death. I want more depth of conversation and closure, but others do not need that. I need to write about it, express it, process it, analyze it, and dig into the questions my heart and soul have. I used to apologize for being like this, but I now have let that go. There is nothing weird or wrong with me for being a truth seeker. It sets me free! It brings me a depth of understanding about people and life that I hunger for. Jesus spoke and lived without feeling the need to get people's approval. Therefore, He was free to speak the truth in love. Pleasing God and being true to ourselves will many times separate us from others.

God made fish to swim and deer to run and squirrels to climb trees. We seem to accept that animals are all different and have their own special qualities of existence. We do not try to make a fish climb a tree or a squirrel swim in the ocean. What a beautiful world this would be if we could look at humans like this and accept each of our own unique talents, purposes, and responses. If we would just stop allowing others to put us in a box long before we die! For whatever we are carrying as our unique gifts or purpose, the world needs. They were given to us for a reason, so share them.

The biggest gift we all have is the gift of our heart. It has great power. You never have to tell it to beat, or love, or feel pain. Those abilities are automatic; they come with being human and alive. Doctors who have done open heart surgery have reported that after such a traumatic operation, when the surgery is complete and the heart is put back into place, some patients have to be told to tell their hearts to beat again. They need help in jump-starting their hearts. So, it was with me. Going through the death and loss and traumatic whirlwind experience with the end of my mother's life, there were days I did not feel like I was going to survive. My daily purpose to be there for her was gone. Add to that the rejection of my family and the loss of my mother's presence, and I was aimlessly existing. One day, I woke up and realized my heart was numb; I needed that jump-start. I thought of several different negative ways to numb the pain and fill the void. But the reality was that I had survived loss and trauma, and it was time to tell my heart to beat again.

I started meditating and putting into practice something I learned in recovery: Close your eyes and envision the most joyful moment in your life. Maybe it was your wedding day, or the day your child or grandchild was born, or the day a vision or dream came to pass. Do you see it? Now, take the deepest breath you can, and feel that moment again. Take in all its love and joy! Next, envision a white light surrounding that moment. Breathe deep. Notice how strong your heart feels. It is like it is going to burst out of your chest. Hold on to it. Stay with it. Feel the incredible peace that comes over you. Empty your mind of everything else and keep breathing deeply and focusing on that white light, that joy. Now embrace all that you are feeling in the moment. Give thanks. Let peace fill you.

"Tell your heart to beat again...Close your eyes and breathe it in. Yesterday's a closing door...you don't live there anymore. Say goodbye to where you've been...and tell your heart to beat again." (17)

Mom and her brothers

Mom, my siblings, and me...1962

My siblings and me...1964

Last photo of us all together...Mom, my siblings, and me...2007

···9···

He Restores

Dear Mom, 5-10-19

So much has happened in the last 6 months and I am sorry that I have not written since last summer. I think of you often and chat in my mind with you now and then but am finding it hard to sit and write. Not because I do not have lots to tell you, but because I need to gather my thoughts and process so I can best put this into words.

I have been dealing with my very sick cat, Sunshine, for the last year. She was as frail and thin as you were when you were sick and howled in pain often. It meant not a lot of sleep for me, and it brought back memories of my other cats and their end of life, along with yours. She was 19 years old and truly the Sunshine of my life! I had had her since she was born. Her mama would not feed her, so I became her mama. I loved it and loved her. I spent every night I was home cuddled up with a book and her on my lap. I was bonded to her like no other animal I have ever had.

I don't believe in euthanasia. The good Lord gave her, her first breath, and He would take her last. I swore that I would never put an animal to sleep. The days of watching her and seeing her in pain reminded me of my days with you over and over again. I held her, I sang to her, I stroked her tiny little head. I gave her drops of water and food and prayed for God to take her home peacefully. She was a fighter, as you were, and hung on and on.

I got to the point that I could not take it anymore and decided to have her put to sleep. That was the most awful experience. I do not want to write about it, I don't want to tell you about it, I don't even want to think about it, and I don't want to go through that again. Ever!!

Now her ashes sit beside the few ashes I have left of yours. I cared for both of you, was committed to you both, nurtured you at the end of life, and made sure you both died with dignity.

My life at this time was really busy, and I did not take the time to grieve Sunshine's death. It happened in the middle of the holidays. A few weeks later, I was heading up to Minnesota again to welcome another grandbaby.

On Christmas Eve Day, I got the call to come stay with my granddaughters, as mom and dad were going to the hospital. I had these little girls all to myself and was going to make it the most magical Christmas Eve ever! We all got dressed up and went to church and came home and made dinner and then adorned my beautiful chocolate birthday cake with candles and sang and celebrated my big day. We had a blast opening lots of presents and taking many photos. We finished the evening by writing a letter to Santa, asking him to please bring the presents to the hospital so the girls could open their presents with Mom and Dad and their new baby. I tucked the girls into bed, read them a story, and said a little prayer with them. I had never felt such joy! The anticipation for them of waking up on Christmas morning to presents and a new baby was overwhelmingly precious. It was the magic that we all dream about, and some remember as children. This Christmas Eve was one that truly was heaven sent!

It's a boy! My night was made complete with the news, and my birthday is made more special because I have a grandson who will now experience a Christmas Eve birthday. There is a specialness to having a Christmas birthday. The world will make him believe for many years that he is being cheated out of presents because they are so often combined as one gift for both Christmas and birthday. It may be hard for him to feel special on this day, as everyone else will be opening presents along with him. But one day, he will grow up and find the true meaning of the season...and then none of the presents, or needing your own special day, will really matter.

Mom, my thoughts go out to you and to my daughter-in-law. You both spent a Christmas in pain and labor...an unforgettable Christmas for you both, I am sure! Though history had repeated itself, some things were different. This baby's father, my son, was there at the birth, and he will be there for his son and his wife and his 2 daughters. So often, when history repeats itself, generational curses take place. I am beyond grateful that this Christmas brought a different ending than the Christmas of 1961, and a generational blessing was born.

I spent the next day sitting in the hospital room, holding my new grandson, and gazing many times across the wing to the room where you had passed. Reflecting again on how the Lord gives and the Lord takes away—and blessed be his name. I thought for a moment about going over and visiting your nurse again. Instead, I hung on to this new little life in my arms and decided to not go back.

Death and loss have taught me how I want to live, Mom. Weeping endures for a night, but joy comes in the morning. I know you aren't going to be the last person I lose, and that Sunshine won't be the last animal that I lose, but the older I get, the more I realize that these losses don't have to be the dark places they use to be. The vivid memory of you holding your hand to heaven and reaching upward and the bright light that shone around your face is forever imprinted in my mind. It is an inspiration for me in dark times to look up, to lift my hands up in praise, and to keep reaching and heading towards the light!

I love you, Mom. Miss you.

Happy Mother's Day!
Kristy

••• 10 •••

Reprise

I waited patiently for the Lord,
He turned to me and heard my cry.
He lifted me out of the pit of despair,
out of the mud and the mire.
He set my feet on solid ground and
steadied me as I walked along.
He put a new song in my heart,
a hymn of praise to our God. Many
Will see what He has done,
and they will put their hope in Him!
(PS 40: 1-3 NKJ)

IN JUNIOR HIGH and high school, I use to write and speak and compete and win awards. God gave me a vision when I was 18 years old that I would someday write and speak again. At that time, He did not give me the vision of my purpose, of what I would write about. It was much like my favorite Bible story and character, Joseph. Joseph saw the promise of elevation, ruling over the land, and his brother bowing down to him, but he never saw the pit or the prison he would have to endure to get to that promise! My pit and prison have been the many years of alcoholism, abuse, and abandonment I endured in my family and adult relationships. I see now that I had to suffer because it was a part of my journey to His promise and purpose for my life. What the enemy meant for evil, God will turn and use for His good.

I have a great passion for wanting to understand people with addictions and codependent behaviors. My upbringing fuels me to dig deeper into these toxic patterns in relationships. I also have a tremendous amount of compassion for those who, as children, have suffered in these households. My promise of writing is being fulfilled, and my purpose to write is to tell my truth. Not to minimize, alter, or deny it for the sake of pleasing others, as I have always done. This book is my truth! It may not be how other members of my family remember growing up in our household, or how they experienced my mother's end of life. But all I can do for my own recovery is tell my truth. Others will have to find their own expression of it. As for me, my heart wants to release my writing for a greater good. For others who suffer and need to find a savior or Higher Power. For those who are at the end of their lives and are needing to find forgiveness and hope beyond this world. For those who need to make amends and make someone's end of life be a peaceful one.

I pray that every adult child of an alcoholic gets to experience a moment in their lives as I did the night I cuddled up with my mother on her dying bed. I pray that you finally get to let out all the years of emotionally taking care of someone else who suffered from the disease of alcoholism and abuse—and just be a child. To be embraced for the years that you were expected to be the grown-up. That you will have that tender moment, where this can all be released in the arms of someone who once held you, and you can sob uncontrollably for all that the disease has stolen from you.

I was 24 years old when I stepped into my first recovery group meeting. I was pregnant with my son and was soon to be a single mom. The father of my son had a serious drinking problem, and it was his mother who first got me on my journey to find some help and wholeness in my life.

My relationship with my son's father was much like my relationship with my mother. I experienced years of verbal abuse and countless promises to me and my son that never came true. His Jekyll and Hyde personality and vulgar, drunken ways were just repetition of my childhood. I never married him. We parted ways shortly after I gave birth. I then spent the next 18 years dealing with him in legal and custody battles, trying to protect my son from him and his drinking. He had gone through treatment several times but had a hard time staying sober. Sadly, at the age of 56, just a little over a year ago, he passed away.

Going back to his funeral dug up my many years of bitterness and judgment. I sat in prayer and reflection of this and found gratitude in my heart that his battle with alcohol was over. And I forgave him. I was sad and sorry that I never apologized to him for my anger and hard heart towards him. Before I left, I reached out to his mother, my son's grandmother. I hugged her and thanked her for introducing me to recovery and told her that I was sorry I never expressed to her son my gratitude for giving me the greatest gift I ever received—the gift of my son. We hugged and wept together for a moment and allowed the forgiveness and peace of surrender to console us both.

Now, after thirty some years of recovery, I have worked with professional therapists and group therapy, and I've taken two trips to Onsite for their programs. I have been in a CoDA (Codependents Anonymous) group and Celebrate Recovery program, working the twelve steps, along with investing in a life coach and conversation coach. The common thread in all my recovery as an adult child of an alcoholic and codependent is to trust myself, give myself a voice, and tell my truth!

I have had to learn to shield myself and not let other people tell me what to do. I have also learned not to play God in others' lives and tell them what is right for them. Only God can do that. I have had to learn to hear from Him what is right for me. I have sought help from several professional therapists and coaches and read countless self-help books. I have come to realize that everyone has their own philosophy and opinion. So, I need to have discernment. If someone's advice is consistent with the many life experiences, lessons, and scripture wisdom given to us in the Bible, then I feel the peace to heed their words and advice. Without that connection, the author, therapist, or coach is just playing God with his ego and words.

I also have learned that I need to show grace to others for where they are in their recovery and allowing them to find their truth. If words that pierce like swords are thrown at me after the release of this book, that is okay. I will understand and will recognize that as a sign of where others may be in their journey.

I still have questions that may never be answered. How much did my mother's drinking while she was pregnant with me affect me? I was born prematurely and weighed just five pounds. My mother said I was two months early. Her story of the fight that broke out that Christmas Eve in 1961, when she was thrown down a flight of stairs and I was born, was major trauma for her. I questioned the story and went on a quest to find the truth of that night. I probed the minds of my father's younger brothers, my uncles. Neither of them can remember a knockout fight or my mom being thrown down a flight of stairs. They do remember my dad coming home, drunk, with his new girlfriend. Do they not remember because they were trying to protect him or their family? Or did this not actually happen? And if it did not, why would my mother make it up? I know she was prone to the Jezebel spirit of mental drama, manipulation, and exaggerating.

Whatever happened the night I was born, or leading up to it, brought her pain, and so often pain can be a drug. When you are in pain, you are not emotionally sober. My mother then became emotionally intoxicated by her pain seven years later, when my stepfather came home drunk on Christmas Eve. My mother chose to unleash her intoxication on me, as her scapegoat.

I have learned a lot about pain in recovery. Pain should fuel us to help others, not fuel our intoxication to wallow in our own pity and become a victim or harm others with it. Pain is all relative. My therapist said to me many years ago that most people's pain is like a paper cut to me. And after years of sitting and listening to many addicts and codependents in recovery and therapy rooms, my pain is like a paper cut compared to theirs. Pain is all relative.

I asked my mother a few years before she died about the fight, as I was still in my truth-seeking journey. She looked at me very blankly and said she did not remember that happening. Really? Did it not happen? Was her dementia a part of her not remembering it? I asked again, and she just shook her head. This is why I am such a truth seeker. The story that was unleashed on me when I was seven years old scarred me and paralyzed so much of my thinking, making me believe that I was anything but wanted. That's part of the dysfunction of alcoholism—it makes everyone else around the alcoholic feel crazy because you never know what the truth is!

All I can do now, is tell my truth, without exaggeration or denial. I push every day to live in truth for my own health and well-being. I do this not only for me, but for everyone in my life and coming in my family's path behind me. Perhaps honesty and truth will help break the vicious chain of the addictions and lies!

I have heard it said and now can see that people are born to look and sound like their parents and die looking like their decisions and the words they have spoken. I certainly have made my share of not-so-good decisions as a child and an adult because of the aftermath of the mess and dysfunction I was born in. I am happy to have found a lifestyle of daily discipline and choices to make healthy deposits in my mind and spirit. I get on my elliptical every day and recite from memory my over 200 Bible verses.

This is my practice of the Swords of Words, in which I battle and slay the piercing words: "You should have died, you're damn lucky to be alive." I slay them with the sword of the spirit, the word of God, and his hope and promises for my life.

I pray and meditate daily, along with listening to great Christian speakers and writers who encourage me. Each day, I relish in being a whole person. Even as a single person. I know my character defects. The chaos and disorder in which I once lived conditioned me to want to control my environment, and I became a bit of a neat freak and perfectionist as a result. Everything in my home has its order, to a fault. I also can have unrealistic expectations of perfection for people, including for myself. When there is a change in behavior in someone, or they do not do what they say they are going to do, it can derail me. The constant change of the alcoholic's mood and the inability to be accountable for their words and actions left a deep scar. I work on this daily. Trust is a huge issue. Getting close to someone requires vulnerability and commitment, neither of which were modeled for me.

I know there are people who think I have become very self-centered in my later years of life. Most of them, as I have mentioned, do not understand the difference between being self-centered and practicing self-care. For years, I felt the burden to take care of my mother emotionally. As a child, I had to learn to take care of myself because she was often unavailable, and my father was nonexistent in my life. As an adult, I was a single mom to a child whose father was just as unavailable and absent. This was all very overwhelming to me. The responsibility of being there and being the sole provider and caretaker for my son, myself, and even my mother, was a heavy cross to bear.

In the last ten years, since being divorced, I have been able to finally just take care of me, my animals, and my business. It is a lovely place to be! Yes, I would love to have a significant other in my life, but not at the price of giving up the peace and drama-free life I have found. It would require someone who has done some of the same work on himself that I have done on myself. Someone who does not want to rescue me or have me rescue him, but would be a complement to my life, journey, and purpose with his own intentional living. Someone who would co-create with me a deeper destiny as a power couple to help others. Someone who is up for the challenge of becoming the best version of himself. I think his name will be Reciprocity.

I have experienced some negativity in just the mention of my writing this book and its topic. Jealous spirits have attempted to slay me and my dream of becoming an author with the authority to speak on my recovery, questioning whether I am really healed. Here is what I, as a Christian and student of recovery, have learned about healing. No healing will happen without the help of the great physician, Jesus Christ. And ultimate healing will only happen when we get to heaven and see Him face to face.

Until then, healing is a choice. Scar tissue from the battles and wounds I have endured is a part of my DNA. Triggers will come. The battle will then be in my will and my mind as I decide which sword to pick up. Will I pick up the sword of the enemy, with his wounding, defeating words, and allow them to pierce my heart and spirit one more time? Or will I pick up the sword of the spirit, which is the word of God, and defeat the enemy with God's promises? Healing is a choice!

Nobody escapes being wounded. We are all wounded people, whether physically, emotionally, mentally, or spiritually. The main question is not, 'How can we hide our wounds?' so we don't have to be embarrassed, but 'How can we put our woundedness in the service of others?' When our wounds cease to be a source of shame, and become a source of healing, we have become wounded healers.

Henri Nouwen

• • •

This is a letter to all you daughters and sons out there who are entering into this chapter of your life with an aging parent.

Dear Daughter,

Someday I will be old. When the time comes, be patient with me. If I repeat a story hundreds of times, please do not interrupt me. Just listen! After all, I used to tell you the same bedtime story hundreds of times when you were little. If I do not understand the latest technology, don't make fun of me. I taught you how to eat, how to walk and hopefully how to live a good life. If my legs are too frail to carry me, help me walk. The same way I helped you with your first steps. And when my time comes to leave you, do not be sad. Help me face my journey with love and patience. I will thank you with a smile and unending love. I love you…Mom! By: Spring in the air (18)

Now, I have come to the close of writing my mother's story. It is also her mother's story, and is now part of my story, and will be a part of my son's story and my grandchildren's story and their children's story and on and on.

Our stories are legacies we leave. We become a part of someone else's story, and these stories cross over generations and states and countries and lifetimes. And in the middle of these stories are threads of "life itself" moments when life itself brings us to our knees. Pain, desperation, loss, isolation, setbacks, and breathless moments that make us wonder how we are going to go on or what that would even look like.

As people come in and out of our lives, we constantly evolve. The human spirit is forced to re-align, to get back up and to keep moving forward so that the stories can continue, so that those behind us have a chapter of hope and a reason to tell their own stories. All of our stories are becoming a part of a much larger story!

I pray that you heed my words through the story I have shared in the form of letters, lessons, and life experiences….

To whom am I writing and speaking?

To you, who has unforgiveness and bitterness in your heart towards a mother, a father, a sister, a brother...

To you, who thinks that someone needs to fit your mold of righteousness to prove to you that they are good enough or holy enough to be saved...

To you, who has lost someone or something close to you, through death, divorce, abandonment, or some irreconcilable difference. To you, who think you will never love again, you will never get over that loss, that wound, that unbearable pain...

To you, who has sought to numb that pain or looked to fill that loss in a bottle or a drug or a relationship or a job or status...

To you, who has sat alongside the bed of a loved one, watching every human ability be taken from them. Feeling helpless and overwhelmed with the wasted years of unforgiveness and bitterness and wishing you could go back and do it differently. Holding on to every word and breath they take, believing that it will be their last, and wanting more than anything for them to hold on...

To you, who wants so desperately to find peace and hope and let go...

The greatest offer I have found for that is the Prince of Peace. Not a religion or a church building, or some pie in the sky belief, but an intimate, personal relationship with the only ONE who, on that very dark night of Good Friday thousands of years ago, prayed for you in the garden of Gethsemane. He was arrested for you. He was tried six times throughout the night while you slept soundly. He was finally convicted by a court of people—people He blessed and walked with and shared with. They struck His head over and over again. They spat on Him. He was scourged with a device that tore His skin off His back. He lost substantial blood. He was given a cross to carry and a crown of thorns on His head. He moved with His cross through the marketplace and was ignored by many people just like you and me. I ask you to stop for a moment and feel the weight of that cross.

He grew weak. It was a long difficult day. He made it to the top of the hill on Calvary. There, they nailed Him to that cross. If you listen, I bet your heart can hear the pounding of the spikes and feel the piercing pain of those nails.

He was stripped naked to cause Him greater shame, the shame that you and I feel when life has stripped us of everything we have and know. He bled and endured and thought of you. The sun was hot. The sweat stung his brow and the flies gathered. The people mocked! But Christ did not respond and God the father watched in LOVE.

His arms and legs became exhausted. His breathing labored as he spoke, "Forgive them, Father, for they know not what they do." It grew dark, dark as death. He could have stopped His suffering at any moment…yet He did not. There was a promise and hope to fulfil! For you, for me, for the world.

His dignity as a man was now gone; his strength gone. But His love as our Savior remained. He turned to the thief on the cross and declared, "Today you will be with me in paradise." His breathing was heavy, for He felt the weight of all our sins was hanging on that moment and on that cross. With that, He raised His head and looked into our hearts and into each of our eyes for eternity and cried out, "Father…My God, my God, why have you forsaken me?"

He then looked up to heaven and proclaimed, "It is finished." And with that, He gave up His spirit and took His last breath.

This man who suffered and died for you, His name is Jesus Christ. There is no pain, there is no suffering that you have gone through on this earth that He has not already endured! I share my birthday with this man, not by accident or coincidence, but because I believe He has a message of hope beyond all this world that He has put on my heart and wants me to share. I believe my suffering and years of pain with my mother and her death was allowed so I could become more like Him. It was only by His miraculous grace that it ended as it did. And now, I am able to share the lessons I learned and the healing and love that came from it.

In this time of desperation, when all we know is doubt and fear, I believe there is only one foundation. I believe in God the Father, I believe in Jesus Christ, I believe in the Holy Spirit, and He has given me new life! I believe he conquered death and that one day, He is coming back.

It is with that hope that I eagerly wait to see the light and to enter His presence and hug my mother again!

• • •

My prayer for each of you, my readers and listeners, is to go out into the world and be His light.

To love deeper.

Speak sweeter.

Give forgiveness you have been denying.

Get out those good dishes.

And if you get the chance, help someone fulfill their final wishes.

And live; live like you or someone close to you is dying! (19)

**TO CARE FOR THOSE WHO
ONCE CARED FOR US
IS ONE OF LIFE'S
HIGHEST HONORS**

••• 11 •••

Thoughts, Scripture Meditations, and a Prayer

AS A VICTIM of much verbal abuse, a lot of my recovery has been to reprogram the hurtful, condemning, wounding words that have been spoken to me over my life. I have also had to learn to tame my own tongue and learn what was healthy, loving, and appropriate to speak.

Many of us have experienced the "verbal vomit" of others on us in the form of the multitude of words—a motor mouth. Vulgar words from the potty mouth. Damaging words from the demeaning mouth. Condescending words from the controlling, manipulative mouth. Sexual, sensual words from the seducing mouth. Gossiping words from the garbage mouth. And even the other extreme—the silent tongue of the mute mouth. The tongue can be an addiction. To hear oneself talk, to boast, to belittle, to control, or to conquer and ensnare.

Words are energy and can cast spells—that is why it is called "spelling." Change how you speak to yourself and to others, and you can change your life. The only hope for the tongue is the spirit of God. It must be bridled and brought into submission by Him on a daily basis. Spiritual maturity will require that we learn to speak fruitful words. Words that build up and do not tear down. Words that are honest and encouraging and filtered by "the fruits of the spirit of love, joy, peace, patience, kindness, goodness, faithfulness, gentleness, and self-control. Against such…there is no law! (Gal 5:22-23 NKJV)

Daily meditating on the scripture verses below renews my mind and heart to be in alignment with how God would want me to use my tongue and choose my words. I pray these verses become a part of your mindful daily meditation and practices.

The Lord God hath given me the tongue of the learned, that I should know how to speak a word in season. (Is 50:4 KJV)

"I create the fruit of the lips; peace, peace to him who is far off and to him who is near." Says the Lord, "and I will heal him." (Is 57:19 NKJV)

Let the words of my mouth and the meditation of my heart be acceptable in Your sight, O Lord, my strength, and my Redeemer. (PS 19:14 NKJV)

You shall hide them in the secret place of your presence from the plots of man; You shall keep them secretly in a pavilion from the strife of tongues. (Ps 31-20 NKJV)

Let your heart retain my words. (Pro 4:4 NKJV)

Incline your ear and hear the words of the wise and apply your heart to my knowledge; for it is a pleasant thing if you keep them within you. Let them all be fixed upon your lips. (Pro 22:17-18 NKJV)

Keep your heart with all diligence, for out of it spring the issues of life. Put away from you a deceitful mouth and put perverse lips far from you. (Pro 4:23-24 NKJV)

In the multitude of words sin is not lacking, but he who restrains his lips is wise. The tongue of the righteous is choice silver; the heart of the wicked is worth little. (Pro 10: 19-20 NKJV)

A soft answer turns away wrath, but a harsh word stirs up anger. (Pro 15:1 NKJV)

Death and life are in the power of the tongue, and those who love it will eat its fruit. (Pro 18: 21 NKJV)

He who has knowledge spares his words, and a man of understanding is of a calm spirit. Even a fool is counted wise when he holds his peace; when he shuts his lips, he is considered perceptive. (Pro 17: 27-29 NKJV)

Take words with you and return to the Lord. Say to Him, "Take away all iniquity; receive us graciously, for we will offer the sacrifices of our lips. (Hos 14:2 NKJV)

Do not be rash with your mouth and let not your heart utter anything hastily before God. For God is in heaven, and you on earth; Therefore, let your words be few. (Ec 5:2 NKJV)

You have wearied the Lord with your words; Yet you say, "In what way have we wearied Him?" In that you say, "Everyone who does evil is good in the sight of the Lord, and He delights in them," Or, "Where is the God of justice?" (Mal 2:17 NKJV)

"Either make the tree good and its fruit good, or else make the tree bad and its fruit bad; for a tree is known by its fruit. Brood of vipers! How can you, being evil, speak good things? For out of the abundance of the heart the mouth speaks. A good man out of the good treasure of his heart brings forth good things, and an evil man out of the evil treasure brings forth evil things. But I say to you that for every idle word men may speak, they will give an account of it in the day of judgement. For by your words, you will be justified, and by your words you will be condemned." (Matt 12: 33-37 NKJV)

Do not let any unwholesome talk come out of your mouths, but only what is helpful for building others up according to their needs that it may benefit those who listen. (Eph 4:29 NIV)

Finally, brethren, whatever things are true, whatever things are noble, whatever things are just, whatever things are pure, whatever things are lovely, whatever things are of good report, if there is any virtue, and if there is anything praiseworthy—meditate on these things. (Ph 4:8 NKJV)

My brethren, let not many of you become teachers, knowing that we shall receive a stricter judgement. For we all stumble in many things. If anyone does not stumble in word, he is a perfect man, able also to bridle the whole body. Indeed, we put bits in horses' mouths that they may obey us, and we turn their whole body. Look also at ships; although they are so large and are driven by fierce winds, they are turned by a very small rudder wherever the pilot desires. Even so the tongue is a little member and boasts of great things. See how great a forest a little fire kindles! And the tongue is a fire, a world of iniquity. The tongue is so set among our members that it defiles the whole body and sets on fire the course of nature; and it is set on fire by hell. For every kind of beast and bird, of reptile and creature of the sea; is tamed and has been tamed by mankind. But no man can tame the tongue, it is an unruly evil, full of deadly poison. With it we bless our God and Father, and with it we curse men, who have been made in the similitude of God. Out of the same mouth proceed blessing and cursing. (James 3:1-10 NKJV)

He who would love life and see good days, let him refrain his tongue from evil, and his lips from speaking deceit. (1 Peter 3:10 NKJV)

The Power of Words

A careless word may kindle strife;
A cruel word may wreck a life.
A bitter word may hate instill;
A brutal word may smite and kill.
A gracious word may smooth the way;
A joyous word may light the day.
A timely word may lessen stress;
A loving word may heal and bless.
Author Unknown

**Two things that we can never recover:
Our time and our words.
Choose both wisely.**

The Swords of Words Meditations

The battle for your heart and mind is real. For out of the mouth comes what the heart is full of. Therefore, we must put on our armor every day with the **sword** of the spirit, the word of God. For it is sharper than any double-edged **sword.** It penetrates even to dividing soul and spirit, joints, and marrow; It judges the thoughts and attitudes of the heart. (Heb 4:12 NIV)

Judges 7:18 speaks of the **sword** of the Lord and the **sword** of Gideon. God wanted Gideon to speak what He spoke. This becomes the double-edged **sword** that is referred to in the book of Hebrews. One edge is God's mouth and what He speaks. The second edge of the **sword** happens when we speak what God speaks. "I am the righteousness of God. I am blessed, I am highly favored." The Lord is going to give victory by the **sword** of the Lord and the **sword** of Gideon. "In all these things, I am more than a conqueror in Christ." I have the **sword** of the Lord and my sword!

Meditate and tuck His words so that they are in every fiber of your being. They will come to mind when you need to draw your **sword** of words and conquer the enemy who wants to keep you in bondage with the old defeating, piercing words that will kill, steal, and destroy you.

Everything starts with speech. Nothing happened in the book of Genesis until God spoke it to happen: "Let there be light." And there was light. God did not build the light. He spoke it into being. The only thing God touched was man, and He formed him. Everything else He spoke. God is waiting for us to open our mouths and speak, to communicate His truth rather than our pain. When Jesus was sent to the cross, He focused on his purpose rather than His pain. Quit speaking the dead language of your pain, even when you are being nailed to a cross. Speak louder and longer than the distraction of that pain and your words will move you out of darkness and into the light!

You will never completely be healed or whole until you change the words and voice in your own head. You must have appropriating faith! Take God's words below and insert your name and claim them and encourage yourself in the Lord. The battle is real...but the victory can be yours in Christ.

Do not be afraid_____. Stand still and see the salvation of the Lord, which He will accomplish for you today. The Lord will fight for you, and you shall hold your peace. (Ex. 14: 13-14 NKJV)

Be strong and of good courage _____, do not fear nor be afraid of them; for the Lord your God, He is the One who goes with you. He will not leave you nor forsake you. (Duet 31: 6 NKJV)

Have I not commanded you _____? Be strong and of good courage; do not be afraid, nor be dismayed, for the Lord your God is with you wherever you go. (Jos 1: 9 NKJV)

Oh, that you would bless me indeed, and enlarge my territory, that Your hand would be with me, and that You would keep me from evil, that I may not cause pain. (1 Chron. 4: 10 NKJV)

The Lord is my shepherd; I shall not want. He makes me lie down in green pastures; He leads me beside still waters. He restores my soul; He leads me in the paths of righteousness for His name's sake. Yea, though I walk through the valley of the shadow of death I will fear no evil; for You are with me; Your rod and Your staff, they comfort me. You prepare a table before me in the presence of my enemies; You anoint my head with oil; My cup runs over. Surely goodness and mercy shall follow me all the days of my life; and I will dwell in the house of the Lord forever. (Ps. 23: 1-6 NKJV)

The Lord is my light and my salvation; whom shall I fear? The Lord is the strength of my life; Of whom shall I be afraid? (Ps. 27: 1 NKJV)

For in the time of trouble He shall hide me in His pavilion; in the secret place of His tabernacle, He shall hide me; He shall set me high upon a rock. (Ps 27: 5 NKJV)

You shall hide them in the secret place of Your presence from the plots of man; You shall keep them secretly in a pavilion from the strife of tongues. (Ps. 31: 20 NKJV)

I sought the Lord, and He heard me, and delivered me from all my fears. (Ps. 34:4 NKJV)

I waited patiently for the Lord; He turned to me and heard my cry. He lifted me out of the slimy pit, out of the mud and mire; He set my feet on a rock and gave me a firm place to stand. He put a new song in my mouth, a hymn of praise to our God. Many will see and fear the Lord and put their trust in Him. (Ps. 40: 1-3 NIV)

He who dwells in the shelter of the Most High will rest in the shadow of the Almighty. I will say of the Lord, "He is my refuge and my fortress, my God, in whom I trust." He will cover you with His feathers, and under his wings you will find refuge;

His faithfulness will be your shield and rampart. (Ps. 91: 1-2, 4 NIV)

For He will command His angels concerning you to guard you in all your ways; they will lift you up in their hands, so that you will not strike your foot against a stone. (Ps. 91: 11-12 NIV)

Though I walk in the midst of trouble, You preserve my life. You stretch out your hand against the anger of my foes; with your right hand you save me. (Ps. 138: 7 NIV)

Say to those who are fearful-hearted, "Be strong, do not fear! Behold, your God will come with vengeance, with the recompense of God; He will come and save you." (Is. 35: 4 NKJV)

He gives power to the weak, and to those who have no might He increases strength. Even the youths shall faint and be weary, and the young men shall utterly fall. But those who wait on the Lord shall renew their strength; They shall mount up with wings like eagles, they shall run and not be weary, they shall walk and not faint. (Is. 40: 29-31 NKJV)

Fear Not_____, for I am with you; Be not dismayed, for I am your God. I will strengthen you, Yes, I will help you, I will uphold you with My righteous right hand. (Is. 41:10 NKJV)

"Fear not_____, for I have redeemed you; I have called you by your name; you are mine. When you pass through the rivers, they shall not overflow you. When you walk through the fire, you shall not be burned, nor shall the flame scorch you. For I am the Lord your God, The Holy One of Israel, your Savior. (Is. 43: 1-3 NKJV)

"For I know the plans I have for you _____, declares the Lord, plans to prosper you and not to harm you, plans to give you a hope and a future. Then you will call on me, and I will listen to you. You will seek me and come and pray to me and find me when you seek me with all your heart. I will be found by you," declares the Lord. (Jer. 29:11 NIV)

"For I," says the Lord, "will be the wall of fire all around her, and I will be the glory in her midst." (Zec 2:5 NKJV)

Who shall separate us from the love of Christ? Shall trouble or hardship or persecution or famine or nakedness or danger or sword? As it is written: "For your sake we face death all day long; we are considered as sheep to be slaughtered." No, in all these things we are more than conquerors through him who loved us. For I am convinced that neither death nor life, neither angels nor demons, neither present nor the future, nor any powers, neither height nor depth, nor anything else in all creation, will be able to separate us from the love of God that is in Christ Jesus our Lord. (Rom. 8: 35-39 NIV)

No temptation has seized you except what is common to man. And God is faithful; He will not let you be tempted beyond what you can bear. But when you are tempted, He will also provide an escape, so that you can stand up under it. (1 Cor 10;13 BSB)

Finally, my brethren, be strong in the Lord and in the power of His might. Put on the whole armor of God, that you might be able to withstand the wiles of the devil. For we do not wrestle against flesh and blood, but against principalities, against powers, against the rulers of the darkness of this age, against spiritual hosts of wickedness in the heavenly places. Therefore, take up the whole armor of God, that you may be able to withstand in the evil day, and have done all, to stand. Stand therefore, having girded your waist with truth, having put on the breastplate of righteousness, and having shod your feet with the preparation of the gospel of peace; above all, taking the shield of faith with which, you will be able to quench the fiery darts of the wicked one. And take the helmet of salvation and the sword of the Spirit, which is the word of God. (Eph 6:10-17 NKJV)

For God has not given us a spirit of fear, but of power and of love and of a sound mind. (2 Tim 1:7 NKJV)

"I will never leave you nor forsake you." So, we may boldly say; "The Lord is my helper; I will not fear. What can man do to me?" (Heb 13: 5-NKJV)

Sword in the Bible

Listen to me, you islands; hear this, you distant nations; before I was born the Lord called me; from my mother's womb he has spoken my name. He made my mouth like a sharpened **sword;** in the shadow of His hand, he hid me; he made me into a polished arrow and concealed me in his quiver. (Is 49: 1-2 NKJ)

My soul is among lions; I lie among the sons of men who are set on fire, whose teeth are spears and arrows, and their tongue a sharp **sword.** (Ps 57: 4 NKJV)

They came out at night, snarling like vicious dogs as they prowl the streets. Listen to the filth that comes from their mouths; their words cut like **swords**. (Ps 59: 6-7 NKJV)

"Do not think that I came to bring peace on earth. I did not come to bring peace but a **sword**. For I have come to 'set a man against his father, a daughter against her mother, and a daughter-in-law against her mother-in-law'; and 'a man's enemies will be those of his own household.' He who loves father or mother more than Me is not worthy of Me. And he who loves son or daughter more than Me is not worthy of Me. (Mat 10: 34-37 NKJV)

For the Lord takes pleasure in His people; he will beautify the humble with salvation. Let the saints be joyful in glory; let them sing aloud on their beds. Let the high praises of God be in their mouth, and a two-edged **sword** in their hand. To execute vengeance on the nations and punishment on the peoples. (Ps 149: 4-7 NKJV)

● ● ●

Are you living up to the name you were given?

The enemy wants to attack your identity—who you are and what you stand for. Your weapons hang on the belt of truth. Do not go to war without truth; it holds up all the other armor. You cannot draw your sword and slay the enemy without it. You have to get honest about who you are and whose you are. Then wrap that belt of truth around you so when spiritual warfare attacks, you can draw your weapons, and claim your victory in Christ.

Take heed to the ministry which you have received in the Lord, that you may fulfill it. (Col 4:17NKJV)

Kristy Orison

Kristy: Greek origin, comes from the word Christian or Christ, which means anointed one.

Orison: Prayer or plea to a deity. To pray. Communication with God.

My Healing Orison (prayer)

Heavenly Father, I come before you with all my heart, for those who are reading this right now who are in need of healing and restoration. There has been brokenness of some form in their lives from someone who has hurt them, with words or actions or both. It took me forever to find the forgiveness you wanted me to give to my mother. I pray that others who are needing to offer this will find it in their hearts to do it much sooner than I did. I pray that they understand that forgiveness is a process, and it is a heart habit. It is a daily choice to release the offender to You, oh Lord. And to recognize that we are all broken people. We hurt others, and other people hurt us. All out of brokenness.

You are the God of miracles, and I give you all the praise for restoration in whatever form you may choose to make the offense right in each of our lives. For each person who is so desperately trying to fill that hurt and wound with something other than You, I pray that You show up in a mighty way to fill them with Your unending love, grace, and hope. That You would take away the exhausting need for acceptance, affirmation, or affection from anyone or anything but You. Fill us with the knowledge that only You can meet and fill our every need.

I am thankful, Lord, for the armor You have given us in Your word, the sword of the spirit. I pray that we may take up our swords daily and combat all the lies of the enemy. I pray that we may tie the belt of truth, of who we are in You, around our waists and live victoriously, knowing that Your shed blood has paid the price. If we claim Your blood, no offender owes us anything. The debt has been paid in full. I pray that each of us realizes that healing comes as a choice. A choice to forgive! A choice to shield ourselves and not let the offender hurt us again. As Jesus said on the cross, "Father, forgive them, for they know not what they do." (Luke 23:34 AMP). May we also offer these words up to you. You are the only one who can forget an offense. So, I pray for the willingness in each of us to only remember that it hurt, for all it was intended to teach. I pray for You to heal the pain, so that we can move forward, with a restored message, for all whom You want us to reach. We pray to be instruments of your peace. May we be restored. May we see Your strength.

May our lips and words be fruitful and pleasing to You, oh Lord. We give you all the glory and praise for helping us to love fiercely and intentionally, for we know we are not promised tomorrow. May You guard and protect our hearts and help us to release them to You daily with pure intentions. May You sanctify us completely and allow our whole spirit, soul, and body to be preserved, blameless, until the coming of Christ Jesus.

In Your son's mighty name, we pray. Hear our cry and our prayer, oh Lord. Amen.

● ● ●

The Good News of Salvation

"The spirit of the Lord God is upon Me, because the Lord has anointed me to preach good tidings to the poor; He has sent me to heal the brokenhearted, to proclaim liberty to the captives, and the opening of the prison to those who are bound; to proclaim the acceptable year of the Lord, and the day of vengeance of our God; to comfort all who mourn, to console those who mourn in Zion, to give them beauty for ashes, the oil of joy for mourning, the garment of praise for the spirit of heaviness; that they may be called trees of righteousness, the planting of the Lord, that He may be glorified." (Is 61: 1-3 NKJV)

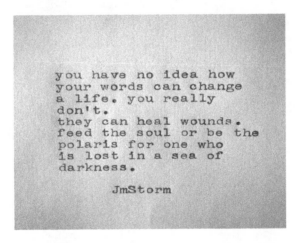

you have no idea how
your words can change
a life. you really
don't.
they can heal wounds.
feed the soul or be the
polaris for one who
is lost in a sea of
darkness.

JmStorm

I have glorified you on earth, I have finished
the work you have given me to do.
(John 17:4 NKJV)

Acknowledgements

I want to thank the good Lord for giving me the words, the vision, the strength, and tenacity to fulfill the writing and publishing of this book. For giving me my mother and all that went with that relationship to create a story that is one of hope and part of His larger story.

I want to give my utmost gratitude to my teachers, therapists, and coaches over the years who have invested in me with their words and knowledge and encouragement of hope, healing, and a higher good. Mary "B" Persinger, my high school speech teacher; Bill Munro, MSW; Dr. Dan Rumberger, PsyD; the late Karen L. Wall, MSW; Christy Kingdom-Knoephler; life coach, Jennifer Agee MA, LCPC; and Mary Schmid, conversation coach.

Thank you to the great Christian speakers and writers I listen to and read every day: Pastor Jentezen Franklin, Bishop T. D. Jakes, Dr. Daniel Dharius, Pastor Keion Henderson, John Eldridge, and Pastor Chuck Swindoll. Your sermons, books, and Biblical knowledge are unsurpassed and are the very breath I daily breathe. Thank you for sharing and inspiring and being a light for the world.

Thank you to my dear friends and colleagues that walked through and prayed for me during some really rough times on my road to recovery, especially in my mother's final days: Charlie Pride, Randy Gould, Fiona Valentine, Phil Eastham, Laura Simmons, and Lenexa Baptist Church. I am so grateful for all your prayers and encouragement. I add Bradley Mosher, Joe McAdoo, John Eller, Mark Kresl, and Brent Chase to this list for your thoughts and feedback in the final stages of this book.

And finally, I thank my dearest childhood friend, Cheryl Albrecht. There has not been a moment in the writing of this that I have not thought of you. You were the wind beneath my wings—and you often still are, in spirit. You were the one, back in high school, who listened to me endlessly as I wrote speeches and had to spend hours practicing them. Every time I had to compete or deliver one, you were sitting in the front row, after first having spent countless times sitting on a bathroom or hallway floor, watching me practice and prepare. Out of exhaustion or our warped sense of humor, we often crumbled into hilarious laughter because the topics I usually wrote and spoke about were so heavy and sad. I would need you and your incredible spirit to persevere through them, and to also experience the joy from getting to the other side of the grueling rehearsals!

We spent hours over-analyzing life and people and problems. and I loved every moment of it. You planted the seeds of faith and Christ in me and spoke prophetic words over my life—that I would write and speak and one day share all that God has brought me through. For all of that, and so much more, my late, great friend...I am eternally grateful!

Cheryl and me, 1979

End Notes

1. "Tell Your Heart to Beat Again." A song written by Bernie Herms, Randy Phillips, and Matthew West and originally recorded by Phillips, Craig, and Dean (2012). Later recorded by Danny Gokey (2014).

2. "The power of life and death are in the tongue." Taken from scripture vs Pro 18:21 NKJV.

3. "How Could Anyone." A song written by Libby Roderick (1988) and recorded by Shaina Noll, Songs for the Inner Child album (1992).

4. "For last year's words belong to last year's language." Quote by T.S. Eliot from Little Gidding (1942).

5. "My Grown-up Christmas List." A Christmas song composed by David Foster (music) and Linda Thompson-Jenner (lyrics). Original recording by Foster and Natalie Cole (1990). Later recorded by Amy Grant (1992).

6. "Stories for the Third Ear." The story of Porky the Porcupine, page 22. A book using hypnotic fables in psychotherapy written by Lee Wallas (1986).

7. "One Day When We All Get to Heaven." A Christian Hymn written by Eliza Hewitt in 1898. Recorded and released by Matt Redman (2018).

8. Exposing the Jezebel Spirit. Narcissistic and Emotional Abuse Articles taken from Facebook group. (July 3, 2019).

9. "Sit With Animals Quietly." Ramblings of the Claury. The Minds Journal. Written by Amanda Rose.

10. "Honor" definition and meaning, Bible Dictionary. www. biblestudytools.com/dictionary/honor

11. "If you are a poor creature," C. S. Lewis quote, Mere Christianity (1952), revised (2001).

12. "Jesus, Take the Wheel." A song written by Brett James, Hillary Lindsey, and Gordie Sampson. Recorded by Carrie Underwood (2005).

13. "Lord I'm Ready Now." A song written by Tiffany Arbuckle Lee and Luke Harry Sheets Walker. Recorded by Plumb (2013).

14. "Come as You Are." A song written by David Crowder, Benjamin Glover, and Matt Maher. Recorded by David Crowder (2014).

15. "Silent Night." A Christmas carol, composed in 1818 by Franz Xaver Gruber to lyrics by Joseph Mohr.

16. "Occasionally in Life...." A quote from Martin Luther King Jr.'s Nobel Peace Prize lecture. "The Quest for Peace and Justice," December 11, 1964.

17. "Tell your Heart to Beat Again", a song written by Bernie Herms, Randy Phillips, and Matthew West and originally recorded by Phillips, Craig and Dean (2012). Later recorded by Danny Gokey (2014)

18. "Dear Daughter," A letter from Mother to Daughter for Mother's Day. Written by Spring in the Air. www.agingcare. com (May 2012).

19. "Live Like You Were Dying", a song written by Tim Nichols and Craig Wiseman. Recorded by Tim McGrawd (2004)

While I am not professionally affiliated with Onsite Workshops in any way, I am grateful to have personally benefited from its programs. At Onsite, you can rediscover you through their life-changing workshops for personal growth and emotional wellness retreats in Tennessee. For more information, you can check out their website: onsiteworkshops.com.

• • •

In loving memory of my mother, a portion of all my book sales will go to The Christ Recovery Center that is a part of the Union Gospel Mission/Twin Cities. They provide hope to men and women facing addiction through Christ-centered recovery. They believe there is hope for recovery with the support of AA, Celebrate Recovery, and other resources. One student described it very well: "We take the Bible in one hand and the big book of AA in the other hand and together work through our issues to recover."

• • •

I pray that if this book speaks to you in any way…you will pay it forward to one who can benefit from it. I love to speak and share my testimony and the miraculous healing that God has done in my life. If your group or organization is in need of a speaker and my topic is one that would be welcomed, please reach out to me at kristy122561@gmail.com.